Copyright © 2024 Mark Chaney All rights reserved

No part of this book may be reproduced, or stored in a retrieval system, or transmitted in any form or by any means, electronic, mechanical, photocopying, recording, or otherwise, without express written permission of the publisher.

ISBN: 979-8-9920979-2-4

Library of Congress Control Number: TXu002194560

Printed in the United States of America

Dedicated

To all creatives and would be creatives. May this book help unleash your creative freedom.

And to Eve Marie.

Acknowledgements

A special thanks to:

Dad, for always being there and instilling in me a great work ethic. Mom, for everything you do. You're the most thoughtful person I know. Lara, for being a terrific sister and friend. Rachael, you helped me find a part of myself which I'd left behind for a while, without that this book may not have been possible. Quinton, Kiel, and Quivaris for helping out on all the film stuff over the years.

Creative Zen

Part One

- The Flow Just Is 6
- Flow vs Force 10
- Forcing vs Not Forcing 14
- Stop Forcing It 16
- Infinite Creativity 20
- Methods To Flow 23

Part Two

- Stop Pressuring Yourself 42
- Don't Let Go, Let Flow 45
- Trust In Yourself 49
- The Mind 53
- Make Your Mind Your Friend 61
- Connect Left and Right Brain 64
- Accept 70
- Overcoming Blocks 73
- Overcoming The Fear Of Starting 77
- Overcoming Procrastination 79
- Beyond Procrastination 84
- Rewards and Goal Setting 88
- Beyond Perfectionism 95
- Don't Wait For Inspiration 99
- The Space 101

Space Grows More Spacious 104
Overflowing 106
When The Flow Is Slow 110
Flowing When It's Not Flowing 112
Flowing When Uninspired 115
Repetitive Works 119
No Creative Bones 122
Finding Enthusiasm 125
Flowing Passionlessly 128
Finding Your Passion 131

Part Three

Idea Creation And Organization 136
Flowing With Structure 143
Rewriting 146
Finishing Projects 151
Multitasking Ideas & Projects 155
Where You Create Matters 162
No Need For Seclusion 165
A Day Off 170
Don't Be Afraid To Lose It 172
Creative Non-Attachment 177
Beyond Judgement 180
Waste Time Freely 183
Beyond Criticism 186

It's Okay to Fail 189
Method Vs No Method 191
When Motivation's Lacking 193
Closing 199

Intro

There's a reason you're here. There's something you want to do, something you want to create; but you may be having trouble getting to work on it, or finding the time or motivation to get started. You want to work on your projects and finish them, but it often feels like a struggle just to begin working on them, or to stay motivated to finish them. Or perhaps you're just looking for a little extra creative inspiration.

Where we often fall short is getting started with our creative work on any given day. That's the hard part. And we often try to force ourselves to create. However, the harder you push yourself towards your creative goals, the further away they often seem, and the harder it can be to start working towards those goals, and to follow through to the finish line.

Do you want your creativity to be a frantic grind? Or would you rather it be natural, easy-going, and flowing? If you want your creativity to be a grueling race through the mud and murk, up river, storm after storm, be my guest. Let it be a struggle. Set this book down and struggle away.

However, if you're like me, you want your creativity to flow and you want to enjoy the act of creating. You want it to be alive and fulfilling. You want to feel inspired. You want to quit procrastinating and create. You've felt the flow and you want to be able to access it whenever you choose. That's the aim of this book, to help you find the flow on a daily basis and inspire you to kick procrastination to the curb once and for all.

Why should I be the person to write this book? Mostly because I believe the majority of books on creativity are missing something—the motivational factor—which is what I hope to bring to the table. Also, because I've created in various mediums and have overcome my intense procrastination with the help of Zen and Eastern philosophies, plus maybe a little Stoicism. I've made a couple dumb movies, a few short films, written dozens of scripts, hundreds of songs, and I'm on my third book, second novel. When I was twenty-one I played bass in a band produced by Train's guitarist, Jimmy Stafford. Still waiting on the video of him playing "What I Got" on stage with us in Vegas. It's believed our guitarist's ex buried it somewhere in the desert…

This book can be utilized by anyone in a creative field, has a creative idea or hobby, or anyone who wants to bring more flow into their daily lives. It's even for non-creatives and those of you who believe you have zero creative bones. You too can find the creative flow, and perhaps end up creating something great, or even many things.

Many of the chapters of this book will end with a brief method aimed at getting you to start on your projects and continue them until they're complete. If you've ever meditated, you'll probably be familiar with some of the methods. They're nothing new, they're just aimed towards bringing out your creative flow, rather than achieving enlightenment; perhaps the aim is for creative enlightenment.

When you're flowing, originality flows through you, life itself flows through you. The more you flow, the more you become a finely tuned instrument, and accessing the flow in your creative life will become easier. Simply by flowing into and through your work, your creativity will come to life.

If you can bring a little zen into it, creativity will flow through you, into whichever project you choose. You simply write it down, play it, paint it, flow with it.

Creative Zen is here to bridge Eastern and Western thought in the realm of creativity, helping you unleash your creative flow. Instead of thinking about your creative projects, it's now time sit down and get started.

By the end of this book, you'll be ready to flow into any creative endeavor with a confident ease. Your work will become fulfilling in itself and you will be ready to start your projects every chance you get. No longer will your art be a war or a battle, it will simply be a flow. It will enliven you and you will never run out of ideas or fear where to go next on a project. You will complete your projects quicker, and without the gut-wrenching and hair pulling toll some of us like to dole out on ourselves.

No more banging your head against the wall.

No more writer's block or any creative blocks.

No more anxiety around your work.

No more procrastination.

No more force. Only flow.

May you find true fulfillment in all of your creative endeavors.

Part One

The Flow

The Flow Just Is

The flow just is. You don't find it, it finds you. Sometimes you can simply start your work, and you'll flow immediately. Some days, it won't come that easy.

The flow comes when you're coming from a blank slate, when thoughts aren't clouding your view and distracting you from the creative work you want to be doing. The goal of this book is to help you get to that blank slate where the flow can easily find you, where you can begin your work and you'll flow.

Once you start accessing flow, it will start happening more and more. You'll be in the flow almost immediately when you begin your work. It will just happen because you'll no longer be forcing it. You'll simply be starting your work from a blank slate where you can concentrate fully on your project.

Starting from a blank slate, you'll see your work with fresh eyes. New ideas will flow, and you'll know where to take them. You'll flow. Your work will flow. It will almost be like jumping into a river when you start your work. You'll start going over where you left off and the current will take you. You'll start being excited by how quickly you can get back into the flow when you start your day.

You'll learn that there is no reason to force. If you try to swim against the current, where are you going to go? You may still reach your goal, but you won't get the same fulfillment, it won't enliven you, and you'll probably be exhausted by the end. Whereas, when you simply allow the current, the flow, to take you downstream, you'll be enlivened by your creative work while completing much more work.

Finding the flow is a little like a balancing act. You don't just find it and you stay there. You are always finding it. The mind will want to swing this way or that way and follow every thought as it passes. If you can balance back to that blank slate, beyond distracting thoughts, you can flow whenever you choose.

I call that blank slate, space. Some call it their center. The reason I call it space is partly because of the methods in this book, such as the analogy of you being the clear blue sky while thoughts are clouds passing by. So the space being referred to in this book will be about the space around, behind, and/or beyond thoughts.

Think of it however you may. I like using space as there's nothing restrictive in it. Space allows for freedom. When you start trying to define the space, you're enclosing it, you're putting walls up. This book is about breaking those walls down. Use it how you wish. Take what works for you in this book and drop the rest.

If you can find space between thoughts, then I can almost guarantee that you'll start flowing once you begin your work. Or perhaps new creative ideas and solutions will start flowing through you immediately.

You allow the flow to happen by finding space, getting back to that blank slate, and being there with your work. Find some space between thoughts, sit down with your work in this moment and go with it. You'll be coming from a blank undistracted slate, so your mind will be able to focus in on the task at hand, and you'll flow.

Simply watch. Find a little space, and the flow will find you. Watch your thoughts pass by. Don't follow every thought, simply watch them. Be the clear blue sky as thoughts pass on by like clouds.

If you've ever meditated or practiced yoga, you may have a better understanding of the space I'm referring to. But anyone can use these methods to find flow.

To flow at any moment, find space between thoughts, sit down with your work, simply be there with it—then it happens—no force—only flow.

When you're flowing, you're not even trying, you're simply creating, simply flowing. It just happens because you're allowing it. If you're writing, simply begin reading where you left off, and I bet you'll begin flowing with new ideas right away. It's all about starting. Starting is always the hardest part, especially when you're used to allowing your mind to constantly distract you. Get back to that blank slate and creativity will flow through you.

The flow frees you from the bonds of time, of past and future. You are one with your work, your creativity, and you're nailing it without even trying. It happens by allowing it to happen, by freeing your mind, by finding some space beyond distracting thoughts, and doing the work. Then the flow can't be stopped. It moves through you. It's like a river as the snow melts from the mountain top. There is no stopping it. There is no stopping you. It's unstoppable, and so are you. So get started and let it happen. Flow into your passions.

Taking a few deep full breaths may be all you need to get to that blank slate—to the space—where you're free to flow into your projects undistracted by mind's endless stream of thoughts.

Find the space, get back to that blank slate, and flow into your projects, large and small, naturally growing and expanding your creative skills as you do.

Flow vs Force

Force is a grind, a friction, a struggle. Perhaps you believe creativity must be a struggle? But if so, you'll be beating yourself down rather than lifting yourself up. If you want your creativity to be fulfilling, drop the forcing, and learn to flow. That's when your creativity comes alive. Force suffocates creativity. It squeezes the well dry and puts obstacles and blocks in your path.

Flow is the way to get true fulfillment from creating. Some moments the flow will be slow and gentle. Other days it will be nice and steady. Then there will be days or moments where you'll be overflowing, and creativity just pours out. Regardless of how the flow hits you on any given day, if you can learn to find some space and bring a little zen into it, creativity will flow through you and into whichever project you choose. You simply write it down, play it, paint it, flow with it.

A lot of people think of the flow state as only those moments where you're completely overflowing with ideas, however that's not the whole truth. The flow state is simply those moments where you're focused on your creative work, where you're basically one with your work; and that's pretty zen in itself. And that's why bringing a little zen into your creative life can help you reach the flow state much quicker and more consistently.

How you flow on a given day will vary. On most days, the flow will simply be smooth and steady, where you'll be able to get your work done with solid concentration. Then at other times, the flow may be slow and gentle, where you're not getting a ton of work done or you're not fully concentrated on your project, but you're still taking some solid creative steps. Or perhaps your creativity is just bursting forth, and your focus is so completely entrenched in your project that nothing can get in your way.

New creative ideas often do come from an overflowing flow —where you don't have to really do anything except jot it down, paint it, edit it, make it, or play it. It flows through you and with you, and we all love that. However, a gentle flow can often be just as fulfilling and a lot more relaxing. A nice steady flow is what I usually prefer.

When you are overflowing with a new idea, simply get as much of the idea down as you can. Then you can come back to it later and expand upon it. The more you flow, the better you'll become at getting the gist of new ideas down, and expanding upon them later will become second nature.

When you're flowing with your work, you'll be energized and ready to take on the world. When you force, you'll often end up exhausted and wanting to disappear from the world.

And if you happen to be thinking about the Jedi Force, realize that's a force they have to allow and work with, rather than against. That force is a flow. Mentally trying to force creativity, that is a grind, it's grueling, it will lack fulfillment, and will likely burn you out.

When you're flowing, originality flows through you, life itself flows through you. You simply let it. The more you flow, the more you become a finely tuned instrument, and accessing the flow in your creative life will be easy. Simply by flowing into and through your work, your creativity will come to life. The trick is to start, and keep starting.

There's a reason you're trying so hard to create. It's what you love. If you didn't want to create, why try so hard? But that very trying may be blocking your creativity. You may be forcing yourself. You may feel like you have to do it, like you must create something great.

When we try to force our creativity and force ourselves onto a task, we often get stuck, and creativity ceases, gets stale, or simply becomes a chore rather than something you actually enjoy doing. That's when we start getting blocks and possibly even burnt out.

You may feel like you have to force yourself to start your work, but is opening up your project and looking it over really that difficult? That's often all it takes to get going, and can be the most difficult part of creating. Sometimes, the harder you try, the harder the journey will be—you'll be running uphill. If you can learn to find some space and flow, your creativity will start to feel like you're merely floating downstream. It won't be a force. You'll just sit down with your work, begin, and creativity will pour out of you. No force necessary, only flow.

Forcing vs Not Forcing

If you're forcing, your thoughts are going to sound something like: "Okay, I've got to do this. Come on. We can do this. Don't be an idiot. Why's it so difficult. I just want to finish this stupid thing. Why's it taking so freaking long?"

Versus not forcing, which goes something like: "Alright, we can do this. Let's start. I chose to do this, so go for it. Once I start, it won't be so difficult. If I can get a little work down now, I'll be that much closer to finishing."

Even when you're not feeling it, you can get some great work done. If you sit down with your work, you can and most likely will get into the flow. If flowing isn't second nature yet, it will become so. Beginning again today is all it takes. Don't put it off. If you've got an hour window, try to simply get twenty or thirty minutes of work done. If you've got all day, just begin and don't judge how much you complete.

Simply by completing any amount of work, you're gearing yourself up to complete more the next time you begin. At first, beginning may feel like pedaling a bike up a mountain. But once you build strength, after several days, weeks, or months, you will reach a peak where it's pretty simple to get going. You'll simply pedal a little bit, and you'll start flowing downhill. You'll just steer the bike. Then, every day will begin to feel like that. You may have to pedal a little to get going, but then it will just start happening by itself. You'll flow on down the mountain with ease.

You will still want to force at times, your mind will. Feel that urge. Notice how unproductive it is. When you force yourself to do your creative work, when you try to hammer it out, how much do you really get done? How difficult is it to start? And how happy are you with any work you do complete? How fulfilled are you, or energized?

When you flow without forcing, how much do you get done? Are you fulfilled and energized? My guess would be that you get a lot more accomplished, and you are fulfilled and energized. I know I am.

And I know that I get stressed and uninspired when I force, which bleeds into the rest of my life. However, when I flow, I get much more accomplished, and I'm energized by it. Therefore, I'm energized in more areas of my life. That's another reason why exercising can help. You'll start feeling more energized, which will inevitably flow into other parts of your life, and into your creativity.

Sure, you can keep pushing that boulder up the road and forcing. Or you can jump into the river and flow. Use this book and the methods to help you drop the boulder and flow naturally, getting more creative work done than you may have thought possible.

<u>Stop Forcing It</u>

When you're trying to force creativity, it can feel like you're beating your head against the wall, and that you have to bust through that wall just to begin. Once you learn to stop forcing and to flow, the wall will dissolve. You'll be able to flow right away, instead of having to use all of your might in the vain hope of breaking through the wall to get started on your creative work. The wall will no longer exist. The blocks will be cleared. You'll be free to flow.

The forcing is the block. When you learn to go beyond forcing, you'll stop experiencing creative blocks. You'll be able to flow around or through any potential block. The walls will collapse.

Flowing is what you did as a kid. But then you began to force things. You were taught to force things. Everyone was. You were taught that you "have to" do things. So that's how you learned to talk to yourself. You had to sit in school all day and do as you were told. You don't have to unlearn anything—simply go beyond mind. You are much deeper than mind. But all western teachings are to train the mind to think in this way or that. And that's fine. The mind is what flows. However, to access flow anytime you want, going beyond mind, beyond distracting thoughts, can get you flowing on a consistent basis—by bringing some zen into your creativity.

At 8000 words into this book, I was thinking all about: "How quickly can I finish. This is week one. I've written over 1000 words in one hour today. If I keep up this pace, that could be over 5000 words a day. That could mean I could be done with a whole book draft in ten days, easy. What am I waiting for?"

Then I realized how those thoughts took me completely out of the flow. Then they quickly turned against me, "Well, what if I can't keep flowing like I've been flowing today. What if I can only write 1000 words in a whole day? What's that, only four pages? How can I only write four pages in a day? I'm used to writing twenty pages in a screenplay in a day. Yeah, it's a totally different structure, and I've been screenwriting much longer than I've been writing books, but still..."

During that string of thoughts, I kind of started to feel bad about my abilities. "Really? That's all I can do? And I thought I was getting the hang of this flowing thing. How can I be writing about it if I can't even flow myself?" Then I stopped, and I started flowing with that very thing. I let those thoughts themselves get me back into the flow. I used them. I didn't fight them, I flowed with them. I used those very thoughts to show you how ridiculous the mind can often be.

I hope that gives you an insight into what the mind will do to try to discourage you from continuing. The mind says, "Look at that long grueling road ahead of you. How are you ever going to complete this? Or anything? Ever? No way. That will take too long. You can't do that much. Impossible!"

The mind goes around and around, following thought after thought, often repeating. But now you're learning how to move beyond thoughts, beyond mind. When you watch those thoughts, they have no power over you. You may even use them like I just did. But most likely, you'll simply want to go beyond mind, beyond thoughts. Then the flow will come, because you're once again back to that blank slate. You've freed your mind, allowing it the space to flow. And flow it will.

Absolutely, you will flow. By finding the space, you allow your mind the freedom to flow. Creativity will pour out of you. You may not be there yet, but don't be discouraged. By and by, you'll learn to get back to that blank slate and flow. And what may start as a dry trickling stream will become a mighty unstoppable river, which will become a great lake or an entire ocean.

How can you try to be in the flow? That very trying creates an impossibility. You can't try to be in the flow or your mind will try to force the flow, which will block the flow.

You just have to allow the flow. Watch, and you'll find space beyond thoughts. Be the vast sky. Watch thoughts pass. Don't become attached to thoughts. Breathe into the space around thoughts—get back to that blank slate—where you can concentrate completely on what you choose. Then you'll be free to create in the moment and to flow.

You're no longer forcing it. You're allowing space for creativity to flow. That's how you flow. Don't tell yourself to flow; don't force it. Come back to the space beyond distracting thoughts, get back to that blank slate, and the flow will come. Your focus will be entirely on your creative work.

Infinite Creativity

There is no end to your creativity, or to life's. Creativity is infinite. There is an endless well of ideas that you can access. You're a bridge, a portal, for an unlimited amount of ideas to reach out and come to life.

I hope this book will help you complete all of your projects with much greater ease. Completing a project should not be a struggle. Allow the flow to happen. Try not to force your creativity. If you can find some space around the endless stream of thoughts, the flow will come. From that space, you'll have access to infinite creativity in the infinite flow.

You don't reach for it. You don't grab anything. You simply notice it. If you can go beyond distracting thoughts and begin your work, you will flow. Instead of following your mind's every thought, watch them from a distance. Be the space behind, beyond, or between thoughts. Then your mind won't be so cluttered, and you'll be able to sit down with your work and flow with infinite new ideas. Your mind will be able to concentrate solely on your creative work, in the moment.

If you allow space to be there, the ideas will come, the flow will happen. You'll have dozens, or even hundreds of ideas to choose from after a short period of time. Just jot down enough of an initial idea to continue it later. Don't think that you have to complete something immediately after the idea comes.

The more ideas that come, the more you'll know which ideas you want to work on first, which ones you'll put on the back burner, and which ideas you'll probably never even begin. Not all ideas are great. Don't expect them to be. Even if something's not the greatest idea in the world, it's still fine to jot down the initial idea, as something may end up coming from it, no matter how ridiculous it may seem. Plus, you'll have it available any moment if you choose to come back to it.

Don't get stuck on one idea and one idea alone. Allow yourself creative freedom. Complete your projects, absolutely. But if another great idea comes along, get the gist of it down so you can come back to it later.

What if the flow's not coming today or at all? Your mind's probably distracted with random thoughts. Observe those thoughts. Watch them. Find space around and between them, then you'll be free to flow.

If you can learn to flow when you choose, your projects will energize and fulfill you. You'll have access to infinite creativity. It's there waiting. Find a little space, allow the space to exist, and you'll have access to idea after idea. And you'll begin to know exactly how to develop your ideas and where you want them to go—you'll flow with them.

Find some space, get back to that blank slate, begin your creative work, and infinity itself will flow through you.

Methods To Flow

In this chapter are several methods to help you get into the flow. These work for me. Use the ones that work for you, combine them, find others that work. Use them any time you need, or simply jump in and begin your work.

The point of the methods is to help you find space, to get you back to that blank slate, where you're free to flow into your projects fully focused. It's pretty much meditating until the flow hits you or until you get back to that blank slate where you can concentrate fully on your creative work.

If you lose the flow and can't seem to find it, don't get discouraged. It happens. These methods can help get you back into it. Breath is one of the simplest ways to access flow. A few full deep breaths can get you right back to that blank slate, where you can concentrate on what you choose.

The ultimate goal of any method is to go beyond it, to drop the method, and to be able to jump in and flow. Use these as you need, but don't let your mind cling to the method. Use the method to find some space, then drop the method, start creating and flow.

Read the following method's slowly as you go through them. Continue any method further on your own, until you're ready to begin your work. Use the methods you like, ditch the others. Or skip them all together and start creating. That's the ultimate point of them.

Deep Breathing:

Here's a simple but very effective method, which you can do anywhere from three breaths to several minutes.

Take deep, slow breaths. Deeper and deeper. Breathe all the way out. Every drop of breath emptied from your chest, from your belly, from every cell.

Now allow the breath to flow in—into your belly, filling it—then filling your chest totally—your ribs expanding.

Breathe out every drop. Let every last drop of breath out; every single little drop.

The in-breath will begin to start on its own. Allow it to fill your lungs, belly, and chest—filling every cell with oxygen.

Then release the breath. Release every drop. Breathe out every drop. Your belly almost presses back against your spine as you breathe every last drop out.

Now, allow the breath to flow in, filling your lungs entirely.

Breathe every drop out… every drop.

Breathe in… slowly… deeply.

Breathe out… even slower and deeper… every drop.

Now, allow the breath to begin to flow in and out with ease, naturally. Just observe your breath. Feel the space that's been created. Just breathe naturally, observing the breath, observing the space. Just watch. Just breathe, smoothly. Continue for as long as you'd like.

Then, when you're ready, sit down with your work. Begin. Flow.

You'll often find that you can hop right into your creative flow after some good deep breathing. Give it a shot.

Stop Breathing:

This method is one of the fastest ways to notice space between and beyond thoughts. It's said that thoughts stop if you stop breathing, where all you can do is observe. You're kind of thrust into the space. This method usually works for me, though it's not one I use regularly.

Breathe normally. Do nothing. Breathe. Just keep breathing naturally, or perhaps slightly deeper if you feel the urge.

Then, stop your breath at any point. This moment. Wherever it may be. No breath in, no breath out. Just freeze it.

Notice how your mind stops spinning. Thoughts stop passing. Notice if you feel any space between, behind, in or around thoughts or the mind—or simply an absence of thought. Watch. Hold the breath for maybe twenty or thirty seconds. Nothing too uncomfortable. Hold it, and watch...

Keep watching...

Now, breathe normally. Thoughts will start coming again. They begin passing by. But once you've felt the space behind thoughts, you'll be able to find the space without this method. You'll begin to easily notice space between thoughts. Then, from that space, from that blank slate, you'll be free to flow and focus fully on your project.

Use this method to go beyond this method. Without any method you'll learn to find the space, with just a natural breath. You'll learn to watch. You'll just know the space exists and be able to find it anytime you wish. You'll be able to recognize it, go beyond those distracting thoughts and focus your mind on your creative endeavors. You'll watch, and you'll find it, allowing space for new creative energy to flow, where you'll be able to jump right into your work and right into the flow.

Try using this technique and then jumping right into your creative work. Breathe naturally. Then at any moment, stop your breath.

Then, begin your work, breathing naturally.

Watch The Sky:

Watch the sky. Go outside during the day. Sit or lay down and watch the sky. Don't watch the clouds. Watch the blueness. Notice it's vastness. Observe all of the space.

Watch the sky as the clouds pass. Don't follow the clouds. Be with the air, the space, the vastness. Stay with the sky as the clouds pass. Breathe the air. No space, no air. Be with the space. Breathe into it. Observe the sky. Feel the space. Let the breath flow in… Let it flow out.

Feel the air, the space. Observe the vastness. Breathe. Allow the clouds to drift past and away while you remain with the vast blue sky.

Keep breathing… Watch the blue sky… Breathe… Feel the spaciousness…

Then, when you're ready, or when an unstoppable flow comes, begin your creative work.

This method can really help you understand the idea of space this book is using—thoughts being clouds passing by—and staying in the space—the clear blue sky.

Vast Blue Sky:

This method is very similar to the previous one. But it's one that you can do anywhere, anytime. It uses imagination instead of vision. If you'd like, use it with the previous method.

Imagine that you're the clear blue sky. Picture the vast blue sky and watch your thoughts. Imagine thoughts are clouds simply passing by. We're so good at becoming attached to each and every thought and following them wherever they go. That's how we lose ourselves. That's how we forget the space and lose the flow. The thoughts take over. This method helps you regain control.

Feel the vastness of the sky. Feel the space. Be the space. Accept the thoughts, the clouds. Let them be. Don't force them away. Don't avoid them. Just feel the space between, behind, and around the clouds. Be the space beyond thoughts.

Be the vast blue sky. Thoughts are just passing clouds. Watch them. Feel the vastness. Imagine it visually, or just feel as if you are the sky. Feel all of the space inside yourself, inside your body, inside your energy field, inside your mind.

Feel the space. Just notice the clouds—thoughts passing by. Don't do anything with them. Rest in the space beyond them, the space you're observing the thoughts from. Just breathe naturally and notice your breath filling all that space. Notice how the breath clears even more space and removes tension and blocks.

Just watch. Breathe. Be the space, the sky. The clouds pass. You remain unchanged. You remain the clear blue sky. Breathe. No denying any thought which may pass. Just remain with the clear sky, the air, the space. Breathe into the space.

Continue breathing into the space, then when you're ready, simply sit down with your work and begin.

Ocean:

Imagine that you're the ocean. Feel the ebb and flow—your heartbeat—your breath—in and out—in and out. No forcing, only accepting the natural ebb and flow of yourself and everything around you. Just let it flow. Just feel.

Watch. Slow down. Feel the ebb and flow. Feel the vastness. Watch the thoughts—waves passing—flowing. Feel the space. Breathe. No denying anything. No forcing anything.

You rest unmoving in the space as the waves swell—totally at ease, because you're not forcing anything. You're letting go with zero trying. It's just happening because you're simply watching and feeling. The tension releases. The holding-on relaxes.

Your mind's not telling you to do or be this or that. You're only watching, feeling, being. Just watch—feel the ebb and flow.

Wherever the waves may take you, allow it. Just go with it by not doing anything. If it takes you, let it. If it just washes over you, let it. Enjoy it. Float with it.

When you're ready, jump on in. Get going with your creative work. Flow with it. Don't force anything. Just start. Begin. Just be with your work, and the flow will take care of itself. Trust it. Trust yourself. Begin and flow.

Start on one small aspect of your project and see if you don't flow right through your goal and beyond.

Observe:

This method's nice to do when you need a short break at any time during your day, or you need a quick refocusing.

Simply observe what's around you. Just watch. Don't question. Simply observe. This method is very similar to some of the others, but with this one, you're not really doing anything in particular. No imagining this or that, only observing, watching, breathing.

Observe whatever you feel like observing. Find some space in or around what you're observing. Observe the area, trees or plants. Observe the building, the layout, the wood. Observe whatever you may choose.

Or simply observe your own body. Just feel it. Feel any space. Feel any tension. Where is the tension? Observe it. Breathe into it. Watch. Feel. Feel the tension dissolve by merely observing it and breathing into it.

If you're fully immersed in feeling, in observing, thoughts won't be distracting you. You'll get back to a blank slate, where you'll be ready to jump in and flow.

Watch One Point:

This method helps you find space. Plus, it helps hone your focus and concentration. If you're having trouble focusing, this method can work wonders.

Watch one point. Be it on the wall, a leaf, a candle flame—your own eye in the mirror—a color, a shape—watch any one point. Allow your eyes to focus only on that one point, totally unmoving.

Notice how your eyes want to move. They keep trying to change focus or shift or refocus. They try to move all around. Your mind wants to go elsewhere. Keep refocusing on that one point and breathe. Allow your eyes to relax onto that point. Let your peripheral vision fade or blur as your focus becomes more and more fixed on that one point.

Breathe into it. Keep watching. The longer you watch that one point, the easier it will be to focus on it. Your mind will quit straying, and you'll be able to remain focused on that one point. If mind strays, simply focus back to that point.

With each blink, refocus on that point. As you continue, you'll be able to keep your eyes open longer. Simply keep focusing on that one point, and your concentration will grow, as will the space between thoughts.

Continue looking at that one point for as long as you wish—be it thirty seconds or thirty minutes—breathing deeply.

Then, once you're ready, jump into your creative work with a renewed focus and flow.

Watch Your Mind:

Close your eyes, and watch your mind. Notice if you feel like you're beyond mind, behind it, or wherever you feel you may be. Personally, I've often felt like I'm behind or beneath my mind. Like thoughts are kind of out in front and above me. It may be different for you. Perhaps you feel like thoughts surround you, and you're in the center. It doesn't matter—simply watch your thoughts. Then, in one moment, you'll feel the space between those thoughts. Then you can simply be in that space.

Again, don't force it. Don't force thoughts away. Don't force the space to grow. Just watch. That's all that's needed, and really all that works.

Watch your mind, like the blue sky methods, watch the clouds pass by. Breathe as you watch the thoughts pass. Find the space between, beyond, behind, or around thoughts. Feel the space. Breathe.

Now when you're ready, begin your creative work and flow.

Release The Tension:

Forcing and pressuring yourself create tension in the body and the mind. We find it hard to release, so the pressure keeps building.

That's one reason exercising and stretching can be so essential to get your blood flowing. It's good to relieve the pressure in your body just as much as the pressure in your mind.

This method is what it sounds like, a method to release tension. It's easy for tension to build inside of us, but it's often not so easy to release. Breathing exercises can be very beneficial for releasing that tension and pressure, and that's the focus of this method.

Breathe into the tension deeply, fully, then exhale. Breathe deeply, slowly, and fully into the tension. Find any space between or inside the tension. Breathe into it. Breath deeply and slowly into the tension as the space begins to break up the tension and release it.

Breathe as deeply and as slowly as possible, with both the exhale and inhale. Keep breathing. Slowly. Calmly. Smoothly. Flowing. Feel the space. Watch as the tension dissolves and the pressure releases. Breathe into the space within the tension. Feel the tension melt away, dissolving totally. Breathe into it. Feel the spaciousness within the tension expanding. Breathe into the space.

If you notice you've forgotten the breath, come back to it and continue breathing deeply. Continue breathing into the tension for as long as you wish, coming back to breath whenever you forget it. Keep breathing into the tension and notice it melting away as the space overtakes it.

Keep allowing the breath to flow. Is any tension remaining? If there is, accept it. Don't force it away. Breathe into it. Let your body relax itself by simply watching, feeling, and breathing into any tension wherever it may be — in your body or your mind. Breathe. Allow the space to absorb the tension from the inside out, dissolving it totally. Allow the tension to melt away as you breathe deeply.

Now, simply breathe naturally. Rest with the space. The breath flows smoothly, gently ebbing and flowing. Sit with the space and float.

Breathe and be with the space. Remain in the infinite space where infinite creativity flows.

Work It Out:

Go for a run, walk, do push-ups, or lunges. Get moving. If your blood's not flowing, how are you going to? You can, of course you can. But when you clear your body of blocks, you get your energy flowing, which can help the creative flow come easier. Clearing your body of blocks can clear your mind of blocks.

Exercise, then relax and cool down. Then, jump into your work and see how much less tension there is and how much easier it is to just sit down and begin flowing. Plus, you won't feel the need to end early to get a workout in.

At any time during the day, take a five and go walk around the block or do some quick exercise; push-ups, lunges, squats, or stretch.

Do yoga. If you haven't done yoga, try doing some yoga. You can release a lot of tension with yoga. Plus, it will help you find more space within yourself and your mind.

Stretching in general, is wonderful. Breathe into the stretch. Let your breath expand and create space within the tension as you stretch deeper. Feel the space.

Now, after relieving some bodily tension with a little sweat, begin and creativity might just flow through you like a river. Or perhaps, do another method or take some good deep breaths, then begin your creative work.

Walking/Feeling:

I believe this is basically Eckhart Tolle's method from the Power of Now. Good book. It was my first step into Eastern thought many years ago. Do this method walking or sitting (or even laying down for some great sleep). Do it however you wish.

Walk… Slowly… Breathe… Observe… Feel… That's basically it.

But for the mind's sake, I'll expand upon it.

Go out for a walk. Walk slowly, smoothly, flowing. Slow down and really feel.

Feel every step. Feel how your feet feel, your legs, knees, and hips. Then your shoulders, your arms, hands, elbows, and fingers. Feel totally. Let your arms swing as you walk. Feel every joint, every ligament, every cell of your body. Your neck. Your bones. Your face. Your jaw. Your checks. Your tongue. Your eyes. Your eyelids. Your ears. Your temple. Forehead. Your entire head. Up through your hair. Feel everything.

Don't grasp onto the feeling. Continue staying with the space, centered—feeling without following the feeling—feel from the space.

Feel the air as it flows against your skin. Feel the sun, the heat, or the coldness. Don't clinch. Don't force it away. Allow it to wash over you totally. Feel it. Allow it to overtake you. Feel as your body acclimates and is energized, almost buzzing. Keep walking, feeling, breathing. If you want, observe nature and your surroundings, or simply feel. Or do both.

Continue walking, feeling, breathing.

Feel the air, the space, the hot or the cold, the energy. Simply feel. Then when you're ready, flow.

Melt:

Allow your energy to melt with the energy around you. We can try so hard to be separate and individual that it becomes difficult to let go and truly relax. And in trying to let go, we can become more attached and tense. So again, don't let go, let flow. Let your energy flow. Let other energies into your energy. Let your energy dissolve into your surroundings, into your seat, into the ground, into the air, melting with other's energies.

Don't force other's energies away from you or shield yours from them, both of which we're very good at. Switch it around, however temporary, and allow your energy to melt with the energies around.

Melt. Dissolve. Simply let whatever you feel flow. Don't hold on—don't let go—just let it be—just feel. Melt into and with your surroundings. Continue melting.

Then, jump into your work and flow. Perhaps continue melting as you flow. Let it be a melting flow.

Whatever you feel, flow with it. Melt and flow...

Free-Writing:

This is a method I had never used until I was writing this book. The first week I didn't use it. But week two, I began to. And after giving it a try, it's one I can recommend.

For writers, just jump in and write, regardless of what you end up writing about. For musicians, start jamming with zero thought. Don't worry about the progression, key or rhythm. Just run with it and see what happens, singing melodies to it. If words come, great. If not, cool.

For painters/artists/designers, just begin with zero concerns about color or what you plan to draw/paint/mold. Just begin, letting your subconscious flow. Allow your hand to do what it wants, let the brush flow. Go with it.

For singers, simply sing. Don't think or worry about lyrics in the slightest. Just sing whatever melody comes through. If words flow, great. If not, perfect. Just flow unobstructed. Record your free-flowing, then later you can come back and add lyrics to the melodies you flowed with. And if some good lyrics flow, you can go back and rearrange them in whatever way you wish.

With this method, you could end up finding something quite special in what you flowed with, for your current project or a future one. Regardless, it can help get you flowing.

Give free-writing a try for a few minutes and see if it doesn't put you in the mood to hop in and flow on your project.

Removing Negativity:

This is kind of a bonus method. Some may find it helpful. I have, at times. I'll include it here for anyone who has pestering thoughts/visions/images that they'd like to clear from their minds. Again, the point of each of these methods is to go beyond the method. Use this method only to clear some space, to get back to that blank slate.

There are several versions of this method, and if you decide to use it, pick the one that's right for you, or better yet, create your own original version. This method is really about realizing that you are more powerful than any thought.

Here's an example:

Imagine there's an energy (yours, universal energy, God, whatever works for you) that begins to well up inside you. Perhaps from your center, or root or heart chakras, or simply from the space you've found, or even from your mind—from wherever works for you.

The energy glows. It glows brighter and brighter. Chose a color or use a pure white light. I tend to use a golden/amber color. Choose a color that makes you feel at peace. Breathe. Allow the energy to grow stronger and flow through your entire body and energy system.

Then it begins to flow into your mind, filling all of the space —overtaking all of the clouds—all of the thoughts. Breathe. Allow this energy to slowly, gently, but unstoppably and powerfully overtake any negative visions or thoughts. Don't push. Don't force. Watch. Allow the energy to overtake the thoughts. The energy just melts and dissolves or burns away any negative thoughts or visions. Do this method for as long as you need to clear away all negative thoughts, visions, or tension.

Simply breathe into the space as the energy glows, cleansing any residue left behind. The glowing energy melts, dissolves, or burns it to ash. Then it drifts away, far from your energy, back to where it belongs, far away.

Breathe, slowly. Feel the relaxation. No forcing. Watch the clouds dissipate. Breathe into the space—totally cleared and cleansed.

Now, let any thought of the cleansing energy float, or melt and dissolve away. Be with the feeling. Be with the spaciousness. Just breathe. Just feel.

Then, when you're ready, jump in and begin working on your project and see if you're not able to create something wonderful.

How To Use The Methods:

The point of the methods are to make getting started on your creative work easier, quicker, and more consistent.

Make any and all of these methods your own. No need to stick with what I or anyone else laid out. Take the parts that work for you, drop the rest. Find other things that work for you. Get creative with them. This is your book, mark it up as you please.

The important thing is to be able to get into the flow when you choose. Of course, some days will be more difficult than others, where you may need a method to start flowing. Then, some days you'll be overflowing, and there will be no stopping your flow.

Use the methods to find space. Don't force the space to be there, allow it. Observe the space around your thoughts. Breathe into the space. Then you can sit down, begin, and you will flow. The methods are to get you starting from a blank slate. The following chapters will really help you conquer procrastination, begin your work with ease, and to flow almost immediately when you sit down with your work.

Part Two

Flowing With The Flow

Stop Pressuring Yourself

Putting pressure on yourself won't help you complete your projects. You won't reach your goals any quicker, and you'll be stressing yourself out. You may complete the project, but you won't be flowing, you'll be forcing yourself. And by now, you should feel that force isn't the best route when it comes to creative work, or really anything other than physical feats.

Leave force in the physical realm, not mental. Let the mental realm be a flow with zero pressure. Don't hold your thumb over the hose to make the water more forceful. Just allow it to flow. The pressure will wear you out, and you won't enjoy the creative process. That's often where burn out and blocks come in.

If you're not enjoying the process of creating, then what are you creating for? Simply the money? I doubt it. Otherwise, you'd be a doctor or financial analyst. Perhaps you are, fine. But why are you creating? You're creating because you love to create.

There's a passion in you that wants to be let out, it wants to run wild and climb to the highest peak. Allow it. Let it be the wild child. Enjoy it.

Once you stop pressuring yourself, you'll get a lot more done with much less stress. You'll no longer be struggling. You won't feel drained after the day. You'll feel energized and ready to enjoy the rest of your day and night. You'll be ready to wake up in the morning and start on the project or begin a new one. Your creative work will become a release, rather than a place where pressure builds. Even if you do feel pressure, find a way to release it, use a method.

Feel any pressure. Breathe into it. Feel it fully. Don't avoid it. Don't fight it. Don't throw it out or run from it. The only way out is through. You have to allow yourself to feel it totally. Breathe into it and space will start opening up and the pressure will release. You'll relax without trying.

Your shoulders will drop back, and you'll feel a sigh of relief. There's nothing to worry about. Find some space. Breathe. Don't force pressure away. Let it fall on its own. Feel the ebb and flow. Be the ocean or the sky, watch as clouds and waves pass by or wash over you.

Simply watch and feel. Breathe. That's all you have to do. The pressure will dissolve. It will release. The space will dissolve it. Be with the space, that blank slate, then the flow will be new.

You'll be ready to sit down with your work. It will start exciting you. You'll flow. You're no longer pressuring yourself. You're just going with it. You're just doing what you love, just flowing. It comes naturally once you learn to clear the blocks away, and you're starting to clear them.

You're starting to feel how natural the flow state is. Once you know the space is there, it's easy to get back to that blank slate. Then the flow is free to flow through you. Nothing is blocking it. You can turn on the flow at any time.

You sit down with your work, and nothing is stopping you whatsoever. No thought can take you away, unless you let it. Otherwise, you let the thought pass and you keep flowing. You're no longer bothered by distracting thoughts. Your awareness is stronger than that. You've learned to stop following every little passing thought or object. You're the vast sky, the ocean, as thoughts pass you by. Therefore, you can focus fully on your creative works.

Do your work. Make your art. You'll start enjoying the process more and more. Keep starting. Keep flowing.

Don't Let Go, Let Flow

Letting go is a bit of a paradox. If you tell someone to let go, that's like telling a stressed-out person to relax and will likely only further stress them out. "How to relax?" They'll start thinking about relaxing, their thoughts will spin around it. So instead of relaxing, they'll be thinking about relaxing, which prevents them from relaxing.

The only way to truly let go is to not force letting go. But the mind doesn't quite understand that. So I say, don't let go, just accept. Accept where you are and go from there.

The mind will want to force relaxation. But you don't relax by trying, by forcing. You relax by going beyond those stressful thoughts. Feel any tension. Breathe and move through it. Feel the tension fully, and it dissolves. Same thing with letting go. You can't force letting go, but you can relax into it by breathing deeply or perhaps using the melting method.

It's possible to think that letting go and forgetting the task at hand, however momentary, will hurt your flow or the creative process. But it won't. It may be what really gets you into the flow and give you a fresh perspective. Always trying to hang onto an idea can end up blocking it. It will have no room to move, so how can it be fresh? Go back beyond thoughts. Watch them, but don't follow them. You are the consciousness, the watcher. The mind is the thinker, thinking thoughts, always busy, never resting. Once you're able to go beyond mind, beyond distracting thoughts, you'll be able to flow with ease.

Your mind will sometimes wants to grasp back onto some thought or idea that just passed by. As I was writing this chapter, I had an idea for another book, and I let it pass by because I didn't feel like stopping to write it down.

But my mind wouldn't let it go. I totally forgot what the idea was, so my mind went searching for it. I could see my mind scrounging this way and that, digging for the idea. It searched where it came from, what the idea was about, where it was going, where it may have gone. I rethought about what book it was about, the new title, why the idea was so important to the book, and why I let it pass without jotting it down. And my mind continued searching for the lost idea.

I could feel the tension of the mad searching, watching my mind go to all these places, racing. It felt traces of the connection to the idea, so it thought that if it pulled hard enough, it would pull the lost thought back. We often think that. We always try to cling on to thoughts. But if it's gone, let it be gone.

I'm glad that I let it pass. As it wasn't tremendously important and it shows how the mind will search and dig insistently. So how can I actually cease the search? How can you?

When your mind's doing something similar to this, trying to hang onto a thought or idea, begin to breathe into the grasping, into the tension. Watch. Feel. Breathe. Feel a little space opening up, similar to how breathing into a stretch or pose helps the tension release and allows you to go deeper into the stretch. Breath creates space.

Take some slow deep breaths. All the way out. Every drop. Every drop from the belly through the chest. Empty every drop out of the lungs, slowly.

Allow the breath to flow in, filling up the lungs entirely—expanding your belly—then expanding your chest—then your ribs—rising—slowly.

Now let it all out—slowly—smoothly—flowing—every drop. Then let the breath flow in, deeper and deeper, allowing oxygen to fill your every cell.

Breathe in and out slowly. No more forcing. Stay with the breath for the entire in-breath and out-breath. Breathe naturally. Watch. Breathe. Slowly. Flowing.

Feel any tension. Breathe into it. Feel the space inside it opening up. Feel the expansion. Allow the thought, the grasping, to dissolve. Allow the breath to dissolve any tension or thought.

Feel the space. Be with the space. The thought dissolves and disappears out into the great beyond, totally dis-attached from you and your mind. Now there's nothing left for your mind to grasp on to.

Come back to the breath. Breathe smoothly. Flowing. It's easy for the mind to get distracted, but you'll start to get the hang of it and realize how to come back to yourself beyond mind's distracting and all-consuming-thoughts.

Come back to the space. Breathe slowly into the space. Rest with it. Breathe out, smoothly.

And begin—for real this time. What are you waiting for? Just start, and the flow will come. Learn to trust that the flow will come. Once you do, you'll know it's never far away, and you can start your creative work, and you'll flow. You'll begin your work anew and refreshed, ready to tackle any aspect of it you may so choose.

It's great to flow. So start, now. The more you start in this moment, the next time you want to start, it will be that much easier in that moment. So start. Flow into and with your creative work. Get into the groove and create something amazing.

Trust In Yourself

Trust your own ideas and creative decisions, and run with them. Don't look for others to tell you if your art is worthy or not, or if it's an idea that can sell. I imagine a lot of your ideas are very worthy, but you're the only person who can really decide that. If you like something, odds are, there will be others out there who will as well. Get out there and create it.

It's your art, own it. I want to hear new original sounds, see new original art and films, read original ideas, and enjoy original projects. There's a place out there for everything. And a lot of very weird stuff can really take off. No matter how out there or wild your ideas are, if you can get your work up to a certain level, there will be an audience for it.

Make your ideas happen. Don't just sit back and say, "Hey, maybe one day if my dream job drops out of the sky, I'll take it, and then I'll do it." Work through your creative pains, learn to flow and trust in yourself. You'll get good at what you do by flowing with it. I'm usually pleased with my work now, but it took years to get here. Creativity itself was always fulfilling, but once you're happy with your capabilities, then it starts getting fun.

Some will love your work, some will think it's okay, then some will think it's total garbage. Everyone's entitled to their opinion. Don't hold it against them. Just keep doing your thing, and by and by, you will become the creative you wish to be. Your work will start shining because you'll be flowing when you make it. You won't be forcing it. You'll simply flow with it. Then it will fulfill you, and you'll enjoy your time spent working on it.

If there is something you want to do, get out there and do it. Create. Take a leap of faith, knowing that even if you're not there yet, you'll become capable at it. And you'll only get to that point by doing it, by flowing with it.

Don't worry if you're not the greatest in your chosen field just yet. You're not going to be when you first start, and who cares? You have a voice. Use it. Don't try to be the greatest in general, just be you. Some will love your work, some won't. You may not even like your work at first, but know that you'll continue to improve. If you can find some space and get back to that blank slate, you'll flow with creativity each time you work on your projects, and your skills will keep growing. You won't be forcing your creativity. You'll just be flowing.

By continuing to flow on your projects, your faith in yourself will grow. You'll start to feel unstoppable, because you are. Your creativity will start overflowing at times, where you can barely contain it.

Keep connecting to the flow. Find some space around thoughts, breathe deeply, then jump into your work, and the flow will find you. You will reach a point where you feel as if you're barely doing anything, but the work and creativity just keep flowing. It just starts happening. It flows through you. Keep starting, keep creating, and you'll get there.

One day you'll start to be surprised by the work you've done. Your creative confidence will skyrocket. You'll feel accomplished. You didn't force it, so it didn't drain you. You let the river make its own path, like snow melting off the top of the mountain. That water has to flow somewhere, so simply allow it. Find some space beyond distracting thoughts, and flow.

Sit down with your work and you'll flow with it. Even in the development, outlining, editing and rewriting/reworking stages; in all stages, you'll be flowing.

You'll know how to get around any blocks. You'll flow around and ultimately through them. The blocks will be dissolved or washed away by the flow, and reaching flow will become simpler and quicker. You'll naturally know how to get back to that blank slate and flow into your work (a few deep full breaths may be just the ticket). Then the flow will be unstoppable. You'll be unstoppable. You already are, you just may not know it yet. You just need to learn to flow anytime you choose, and you're going to.

We want to see your ideas come to life. We humans love art. We love consuming it, almost above all else. We want more of it. We want your art to come to life so we can enjoy it. We want to see new creativity. Don't be afraid to put your ideas out there. Trust in yourself. Trust in your growth. Know that you'll continue to improve. The more you flow, the quicker you'll master your craft, and the more you'll enjoy it. If you can flow, your creativity and skill will continue to grow—and you can absolutely flow.

The Mind

What are you thinking about? Why? Why does it keep spinning around your mind? How do you stop it?

First off, don't stop your thoughts. Stop trying to stop them. Why should you not forcibly stop thoughts? Isn't this whole space thing about going beyond thoughts? How can you go beyond thoughts if you don't stop them?

Thoughts are always going to be roaming around, so forcibly stopping them won't help. That's often the natural reaction to try to move beyond thoughts, but the flow flows through your mind, so stopping thoughts will inadvertently block the flow.

So what to do? Simply watch. Observe your mind, your thoughts. Find space in your mind between and behind thoughts. Rest in the space as thoughts pass like clouds. Then the flow is free to flow through you and into any creative project you choose.

What's this whole going beyond thought/mind thing?

If you haven't heard of this kind of thing or experienced it, here's the gist: Nearly all Eastern philosophies and religions say that you are not your mind, that you are who watches the mind—who observes—mind is what judges and divides. That the nature of mind is duality. "This is good, that is bad. This thought's good. This thought's bad. That person's good. That person's bad."

Eastern philosophies say that you're the one behind or beyond those thoughts or judgements. You're the one who experiences.

It's not quite, "I think, therefore I am."

It's more, "I am, therefore I think."

Mind is simply what tries to make sense of it all. Judgement was the mind's survival mechanism. You can't just expect to shut it off. You must accept its ways. Then you'll learn to go beyond mind, rest in the space, and flow with creativity and with life.

Watch your mind, your thoughts. Observe them. Find space between/beyond thoughts. Feel the space. Why do you keep grasping onto a thought, following it as it spins and jumps from tangent to tangent?

Just watch. Find and notice any space behind the thought, then find space between thoughts. Watch your mind's grasping. Observe and breathe. That's the only thing you have to do to start moving beyond thoughts and get back to that blank slate where the flow state is easy to reach.

It sounds easy, right? The concept is. But mind is quite the trickster. It will get stuck on thoughts about dissolving the other thoughts and start spinning with those thoughts, then it will spin onto something else, then something else. Then it will jump back to other tasks you need to do, think about this person or that, some problem of the past, some embarrassing moment, or some future triumph once all your work is done. It will spin, it will jump, it will flip, twist, turn and roll.

The mind is basically a perpetual motion machine. And it's a brilliant instrument. But without being able to go beyond its ramblings, it can get rather exhausting. And it will often block your creativity.

Having all those thoughts roaming around, never-ending, can naturally make us want to control our minds. And we often do try to control our minds. We want to control our thoughts and think only pleasant and helpful thoughts, so we force the bad thoughts away. We cling onto the good happy thoughts with positive affirmations and mantras.

Yes, good thoughts are certainly nicer than bad thoughts. But forcing yourself to stay in these specific parameters will block your freedom. If you're trying to control your thoughts, you'll be creating blocks. The way through to creative freedom is by going beyond all thoughts, bad and good. The space beyond all thoughts, beyond mind, is where creativity flows through. Because that's when your mind is free to focus and flow on what you choose.

Mind can be brilliant, and we are using our minds when we flow. But we often let its constant thoughts get in our own way. Being able to guide your mind and work with it rather than against it, that's when the magic starts happening on a very real and regular basis. Free your mind by going beyond thoughts, then focus the mind on whatever creative task you choose. Then you'll flow. The mind will be focused totally on the task at hand and creativity will pour through you.

Once you learn to go beyond mind, get back to that blank slate and flow, you'll no longer be fighting yourself. You'll no longer judge yourself. You'll no longer be wearing yourself out with long strings of thoughts upon thoughts upon thoughts, which are keeping you from doing what you want. You'll notice the distracting thoughts, take a few deep breaths, and begin your work.

When you learn to find space beyond thoughts, you'll simply be able to jump into your work and let your mind flow freely with brilliance into your projects.

The real goal of this book is to get you to where you can simply sit down with your work, begin, and you'll flow. But unless you've experienced going beyond mind any time you choose, then it will probably be difficult to just sit down and concentrate on your work. You'll likely have many thoughts in your way, buzzing around, and your natural reaction will be to try to shove or tug them away and force yourself to get to work. But that's not going to clear those thoughts from your mind. Force won't help. Accept that those distracting thoughts are there. It's fine. The mind is extremely useful, it's just most often filled with excessive non-stop thoughts which can make it difficult to get to work on your projects.

To make the best use of the mind for your creative endeavors, learn to go beyond it, beyond thoughts. Mind is naturally clingy. Let it be, just notice it. Don't fight against it. Notice how mind clings to a thought for dear life and never wants to let it go. It wants to follow the thought everywhere, tangent after tangent. But it's okay to let it go. Hanging on is where we get stuck and where many of our blocks come from. We simply can't let go, nor do we want to. We want to follow and cling to a thought until its end, but there won't be an end, or mind will simply jump to another tangent. It will cling to that thought, then the next and then the next, and on and on.

That constant hanging on becomes a weight weighing you down, or a bondage holding you down, and you stop being able to roam freely. There's no space. The walls are closing in. But in truth, they're not. There's all the space in the universe. Only thoughts are clouding your view. There's a huge vastness in you, in which infinite creativity will flow like a spring if you can allow the space for it to flow. You do that by observing your mind, your thoughts, and finding the space beyond, behind, between, and around thoughts—by getting back to a blank slate.

Once you learn to go beyond mind, infinite creativity will flow like a spring. If you can learn to observe your mind, observe your thoughts and breathe deeply, you'll create the space needed for creativity to flow through. It will pour through you and into your work. Your creative work will no longer be a struggle, it will simply be a flow.

Don't get stuck on thoughts about where the flow comes from, whether it comes from your mind, or from beyond mind, from infinity, the collective unconscious, or any of that. Where the flow comes from doesn't matter. That's just a thought about a thought about a thought. It doesn't matter where the flow comes from. The important thing is to flow and how to access flow easier. You've felt the flow. Maybe recently, perhaps not since you were a child. Wouldn't it be great to be able to flow any moment you want?

Perhaps one thing holding you back is how you talk to and treat yourself. Do you treat your mind like an enemy or as a friend? Nearly everyone treats their mind like an enemy whom they have to control. You don't try to control your friends. You accept them. You enjoy their company, but let them do as they please.

And you're stuck with your mind, so why not make it your friend? Who wants an enemy walking around with them every second of the day? No thanks. But still, that's what ninety-five percent, if not ninety-nine percent of us do. I'm very guilty of that myself.

It's easy to mistreat ourselves and our minds. Nearly all of us do it. But we don't have to. Wouldn't you rather be friendly to your mind and have your mind be helpful to you, rather than being stern dickheads to each other?

If you poke the mind, it will poke you back. If you accept it, it will accept you. It's really a mirror. Work with it, and it will work with you. Work against it, and it will work against you. Force it, and your inner child will run, hide, and toss distraction after distraction your way.

It's not about getting rid of bad thoughts and having positive affirmations. Yes, it's important to change the way you talk to yourself, and maybe you do need some affirmations to help improve your relationship with your mind. But then the mind will want to get stuck on the affirmation. It becomes a mantra repeating. As Osho says, "mantras are just a deadening of the mind."

Mantras and affirmations will block your mind's freedom, which will inevitably end up blocking the flow. So, can affirmations be helpful? Sure, maybe at the beginning. But continuously using them will once again become another block. It's not forcing your mind to stop, but it's forcing your mind to stay in one type of thought, "stay in this bubble, don't go outside, outside is dangerous, stay." That's like you're talking to your pet. You're telling it what to do. You're not allowing it to be. That will only restrict your creative freedom and your flow.

Mind restricted, equals flow restricted. That again may sound contradictory since this book is all about going beyond mind to access the flow. But again, you're not forcing your thoughts to stop or forcing mind to stay in this quadrant or that, you're letting it be, you're giving it the freedom to roam, you're merely watching it. You're observing your thoughts, and finding the space between, behind, and beyond them. You're simply being in the space —observing—being—breathing. Then the flow is free to pour through your mind and into your creative work, because it's no longer distracted.

Make Your Mind Your Friend

We're very good at pressuring and forcing ourselves, almost fighting ourselves, to work towards our creative goals. But beyond that is a much greater peace. If you can make your mind your friend, your struggle to create will quit being a struggle. It will become a flow.

Try not to fight your mind or to pressure it, shun it or force it. Let it be. Accept it.

Can the mind be annoying at times? Of course. But it's also pretty awesome and crafty at others. It's incredible and ridiculous. Accept it. Once you accept it and start treating your mind as a friend rather than an enemy, it will do the same. You'll be friends. You should be. Mind is quite amazing.

Use your mind to help get into the flow. The mind is an instrument, use it, take care of it, fine-tune it. Then let it be. Your mind is a very powerful ally if you treat it as such. If you treat your mind as an enemy, an enemy it will be. Treat it as a good friend, and things will go much smoother. You'll stop fighting yourself and forcing. You'll start flowing quicker and easier. You'll be able to simply sit down and begin.

Accept mind totally. Even all its fears and desires. Accept them. Don't force them away. You're not perfect? So what. Nobody is. Nobody's mind is. Don't judge it. Don't judge yourself. If anything, judge others. But then again, maybe don't do that either. But we all do. We're not perfect. Which is perfectly fine. Perfection feels plastic. We're real. Accept your mind as it is and learn to work with it rather than against it. Give yourself rewards. Learn to talk kinder to yourself. Learn to celebrate small accomplishments.

Allow your mind to be. Accept it. Find the space in and around your thoughts. Watch it. Jump into your work, and allow your mind to flow—allow all of existence to flow through your mind. Let it pour out. Don't pressure it. Don't squeeze it out. Simply allow the river to flow however it may.

Use your mind to focus, not allowing incessant thoughts to distract you. From the space, a blank slate, you're able to focus on what you want, and your mind will flow into your work, undistracted by random thoughts.

Take some deep breaths. Or use some other method. Watch your thoughts. Watch them float past. Watch them dissolve. Be the clear blue sky. Then there's space to play—for your mind to focus and flow. Jump into the river and go with it. You've been there before. You know the feeling. Figure out how to get back to it.

The more you flow, the easier it will be to flow. You'll be able to access it at basically any moment. You'll know there's no need to fight for it or to fight your mind, to force. Your mind is now your friend. Left brain structures, allowing the right brain to fill in the blanks. You hop into the flow fully-armed with the tools you need to create your work—to start and keep starting—to edit and rewrite/rework—to finish.

You'll have the confidence to keep starting, which will lead to finishing—no force necessary. You'll simply know how capable you are and how easy it can be to access the flow. And once you find that easy access, your fulfillment will become greater and greater, and your skills will match your flow.

Your self-doubt will fade. It already is. Because there's nothing to doubt. If you can flow, your work will take on a life of its own. The magic will happen—not all at once—not all in one sitting. But by and by, your work will begin to seem like it completes itself as you flow with it, and it will be fresh and alive.

Once you're able to flow into your work whenever you choose, your creative work won't be work anymore, it will simply be a flow. Then an unbreakable confidence will start to build in you, and you'll know exactly where you want to take your art.

Connect Left and Right Brain

One thing that can really help you become a more flowing and prolific creative is to learn to get your left brain and right brain working together. Often, creatives believe that using their left brain isn't creative and that it gets in the way of their right brain. However, using use your left brain to structure and make some simple decisions can free your right brain to flow, simply because you won't have to stop and think about where you want to go with your art.

Using the left brain's structure as a guide will often enhance your right brain's creative flow, rather than diminish it. Don't be afraid to let your left brain lay out some groundwork for your right brain to fill. It will likely open many creative avenues. You'll flow through the structure which your left brain laid out. The right brain will expand upon the structure and will build its own, branching out in endless ways while flowing in the moment. Or perhaps, you'll instinctively want to go another direction.

While developing your story or idea, use your left brain to structure and to ask questions. Then allow your right brain to fill in the gaps and answer the questions. Select the best answers with your left brain. Ask more questions to give more depth. Then once again, use the right to fill in the gaps. Same with editing and rewriting.

You can get a flow going between left brain and right brain, a back and forth, ebb and flow, like the ocean. Let the right brain flow in and around the structure the left brain lays out. And if you want to flow in a different direction, that's perfectly fine. Don't worry about coloring inside the lines. Lines are only guides, not absolutes.

That's how you can guide the flow. You can use your left brain to pick the basic direction, then let the right brain flow, creating its own path down the general direction you have chosen and laid out.

For long form content, let your right brain loose with the help of a little structure from your left brain. You'll be able to complete your entire first draft while flowing with your right brain, without having to stop and think about where to go next.

If you like an idea, write it down. Then start developing it. Ask yourself questions about it with your left brain, and let your right brain flow with answers. Don't judge them. That's brainstorming. Use your left brain to pick your favorite ideas and answers and run with them. Ask questions about your favorites and develop them further.

Say you want to write a novel or a screenplay, where to begin? Simple brainstorming. Maybe lay out some general structure with your left brain. Then let your right brain brainstorm and come up with a million ideas (well a half-dozen or few). Ask questions about those answers. Where are the conflicts, etc.?

Answer the questions with your left brain. Select the best with your right. Then asks more—ebb and flow—the ocean tide.

Here's a way to complete any long writing project: Left brain outlines—right brain flows through and around the outline to complete the first draft. Left brain goes back to mark up the rough draft. Right brain rewrites based off the edits. And on and on, ebb and flow, then one day, you're happy with it, and it's done.

You're simply flowing into each aspect, which allows the next aspect to flow easier. Flow onto the task at hand and your work will begin to feel like it's finishing itself as you take one step at a time.

We tend to think that the right brain is what flows. However, the left brain flows naturally as well. It's simply more of a selector than what we often call creative. Use your left brain's natural problem solving tendencies to make your creative work better, and easier. The more you access the flow with your right brain, the easier it will be to flow with your left brain. And flowing with your left brain will make the right's job much easier—perhaps totally freeing your creativity.

Don't think that your left brain can't flow, or that it's not a flow when you're using it. If you're forcing it and struggling against it, it won't be a flow, true. But you can learn to flow with your left brain rather than forcing it. You simply jump in and get to organizing, editing and selecting.

That's what the left brain does naturally. Let it do its thing—let it judge and separate the wheat from the chaff. Select the things you love and mark out or erase what you don't, or learn from it for next time.

The left brain can create the structure/space for the right brain to do its magic, thus making the left brain very important. The left brain builds the foundation and structure, which is often sparked by one small idea from the right brain. Once you have an idea that you want to develop, allow the left brain to flow, naturally structuring and selecting.

Your left brain doesn't hinder creativity, it allows it to flow freely—it frees your right brain to flow. That's how you can become prolific. And oddly, it enables you to break the rules more freely. How are you going to break the rules if you don't know what they are? Allow your natural rebel to flourish.

Trust that your right brain can find infinite possibilities to fill the spaces and structures laid out by the left brain, expanding and enhancing them. And if you want to smash right through the structure created by the left brain, do it. Flow with it—left brain lays out the general direction—right brain flows into and through it. Flow with the right brain, and edit with the left.

If you're only a right-brain creative, you may be holding yourself back and creating more work for yourself by not planning, organizing, and laying things out a little bit. And if you try to write a feature-length script or a novel without structure, you're going to have a heck of a lot of rewriting work cut out for yourself.

With this book, there was very little organization before I wrote the first 13,500 words. I had named around 20 chapters, but they weren't in any order. I had a general idea of where I was going to take the book. But at 14,000 words, I figured, "Hmm, it's probably about time to get my left brain involved to do some organizing."

So that's what I did the morning I wrote this chapter. I organized the chapters into three parts, plus a quick intro and closing. And once the book had some organization, my right brain was free to go in and add depth and new ideas to what I laid out with my left brain, along with creating new chapters.

Sometimes the best things do come to you without any direction, they just flow through you. But don't be afraid to go back to edit and structure with your left brain, getting the idea to where you really want it to be.

If you're rewriting something, all you have to do is begin reading. You'll automatically know what you want to change, fix, expand, or delete. That's how the left brain flows. Allow it to naturally edit your work. Same with film editing, music, and design—with anything you're reworking.

Once this begins to make sense, stop thinking about the left and right brain. It's nothing to be concerned about. Just don't hold back on creative possibilities by restricting yourself to only using your right brain. Your left and right brains naturally support each other. Start using all of your creative tools.

Accept

Accept yourself as you are and where you are as a creative, as well as personally and professionally. The only way to truly grow is to accept where you are, knowing you'll continue to improve. We always want to judge ourselves. Accepting isn't something we naturally do with ease, but it can be once you start consciously doing it.

Just notice when you start judging yourself. You're not a total master at your given job or hobby yet? Good. You've got room to grow. This is a journey, not a pit stop. Maybe you feel like you used to be a master at your craft, but you're not happy with your recent work. Well then, you most likely stopped flowing and began trying to force your creativity. Accept that. Accept where you are. Learn to flow anew, and inspiration will come.

Maybe you're not as into this project or medium as you used to be, but you still want to continue doing it. Then perhaps you'll need to use the methods a little more to reach the flow—find one that works best for you—or remember to take a few deep breaths when you sit down to start your work. Accept where you are.

Today, maybe you're not flowing like you were yesterday, or last year, or when you were a kid. Who cares? Stop judging yourself for it. That's the only thing getting in your way — or just all the thoughts clouding your flow. If you accept yourself and your work, you'll be capable of going back and doing what it takes to make the project its best and most alive during the editing/rewriting phase. You'll flow with it.

If you're judging and forcing while you're creating, of course your work's not going to be its best or very fulfilling. How could it be if it has no space to live and breathe? Don't strangle it. Give it space. Give it room to breathe and grow, and yourself.

Find the space in yourself, beyond thoughts, and allow space to be in your project—metaphorically and perhaps even literally. Maybe you're trying to jam too much into too small of a space and trying to make every little thing perfect. But if you try to smooth out every little edge, what you'll probably be left with is an overproduced pop song. Real art needs a little dirt. Imperfection is okay. Perfection often makes things lifeless. Be great. Don't be perfect.

Don't judge your work when you're flowing. That will stop the flow. You can edit it later. Just flow with it now, and I bet there will be many pearls in it, which you can expand on later, or even in the editing phase. Or, simply combine the best parts, especially in music.

Don't judge the creating or editing you're currently doing. Simply do what feels right and makes sense in that moment. That's why for rewriting, I like to mark up a draft on my iPad in Adobe Acrobat. So when I go to do the actual rewrite, I'll have the original work and the editing notes to choose from. Then I can choose whichever I like best, or perhaps something even better will flow through. Or perhaps the original was the best? It's up to you to decide, and that deciding will become second nature.

Simply accept yourself and where you are. Simply be yourself and do your work in your own unique way. Accept yourself as you are and allow yourself to grow. Don't force growth. Allow it. Growth happens without any trying or thought—by merely doing and flowing.

Accept your flaws and your fears. If you can learn to accept yourself and where you are with your creativity, you'll stop giving your mind anything to fight against. And you'll stop judging yourself. You'll simply flow. Don't only accept your perfections. Accept your good and your bad. Don't try to perfect those imperfections. Simply accept them. Once you do, you can develop the skills to overcome those imperfections (i.e. for myself: lighting and audio in filmmaking).

Breathe and flow into where you are. Be the space—here—this moment. Breathe. Breathe deeper. Breathe every drop out. Flow. Accept where you are, and keep starting.

Overcoming Blocks

Writer's Block? I don't even like using the term. The mind is a powerful thing. It can latch onto anything. If you struggle for a few days, you may feel as if you can't get out of it, similar to slumps with athletes. But that's because you're latched onto it, you're clinging. You're afraid that you can't do it, that you've run out of ideas, that the well is dry. But nope, you've simply lost access to it for the moment. The well is never dry. Your mind's most likely overcrowded with distracting thoughts—nagging and gnawing at you—and you're following them, allowing them to have power over you.

If you can find a little space around thoughts, you will get the flow back, and the well will open right back up. You'll once again be starting from a blank slate. Writer's block will become an unheard-of relic. Idea after idea will flow forth. Choose your favorites and run with them. You'll simply be able to sit down with your work and get rolling.

Your left brain will support your right, your right will support your left. You'll work smoothly, with very minimal resistance. You'll stop letting unproductive thoughts distract you from what you want to be creating. You'll go beyond thoughts and get back to that blank slate where you'll be able to concentrate fully on your creative work.

You'll be enticing yourself with rewards of fun, relaxation, or goodies. But you won't even need them. They'll just be icing on the cake. To overcome what some would call writer's block (I'm going to call it flow block), all you need to do is find space behind your worrisome thoughts and come back to yourself, to that blank slate.

Or maybe you just need to get your mind off of your current project for a moment. Go exercise and really push it. Work on another project or a hobby. Read something inspiring or enlightening. Go to a yoga class. Meditate. Perhaps do a cleansing method.

Don't allow news and current events block you. Don't let any of that bring you down or block your flow. Bring your magic into the world. Create a new idea that will change lives. Create an inspiring story to bring people together rather than forcing them apart. Or simply create something fun and ridiculous. That's what I usually prefer. Simply create, regardless of what it may be.

Watch the mind. Find space within or around thoughts, jump into your work, and flow. You observe; mind thinks. If you can watch thoughts float on by while you keep observing, you'll free yourself from any blocks and free your mind to flow into your work. And flow it will. Your mind flows, you simply have to learn to give it the space to concentrate and flow into your work, instead of following its every distraction.

If your flow is blocked, you've probably just got a case of mind phooey, and we now know that if you want to get in the flow, you've got to release the mind phooey. Do that by going beyond the mind phooey—the clouds, the thoughts—the mind phooey. Go beyond them. Return to yourself behind the clouds.

Your mind wants to latch onto each thought with all its might. But you now know that's just a chain holding you down—a dam blocking your river of flow—just mind phooey. Release the dam and let the river flow.

Watch your thoughts, see those chains, then they'll lose their power over you. Just by observing them, they will dissolve. The flow will breakthrough and wash the chains and logs away. Then by and by, your river of flow will become an ocean which those old chains and dams could never block, mind phooey be damned.

It will be an almost free state of flow. Nothing will be able to block you anymore, and if it tries, you now know how to go beyond the blocks and unleash the flow. That's how you become a prolific and unstoppable creative. That's when the magic starts flowing through you and doesn't stop. No block can get in your way, at least not any that you can't simply wash away with a little observation.

You can start using your mind to break those chains. Use some Mind Fu to break the mind phooey. Let the space be there. Be the space. Then the river will start flowing through you whensoever you choose.

Even a thought about a thought about a thought is still a thought, and once again, you're caught. Except now you're not, because you now know how to get uncaught.

Yes, screw that sentence, but true. And maybe two or three of you will find it amusing or think it's cute. This whole mind-phooey stuff's a little silly, but it kind of makes me laugh, and also makes some sense.

Truly, to go beyond mind phooey, all you have to do is find some space beyond, between, and all around the mind phooey. Then, from the space beyond the mind phooey, the flow is free to flow.

Overcoming The Fear Of Starting

The fear of starting is one of the biggest causes of procrastination. It's not really a fear. It's more of an avoidance, or perhaps a fear of it taking up too much free time.

"It will be too much work. I don't have enough time. One day I'll get it done. This will take forever."

These are just excuses. Choose to start. Don't fear starting. There is nothing to fear. You just have to break through that initial wall, and the more you do, the easier it will be to break through it. Then one day, there won't even be a wall there. At most, there will be a bit of a haze to clear away. But other than that, you'll be free to jump in and flow.

Read The Now Habit if you really have trouble beginning. It was one of the most important things I read to become somewhat prolific. It's about going from a procrastinator to a producer—about choosing to start, over saying you "have to"—creating a schedule built around rewards and what you like and want to do, finding realistic time to work on your projects, instead of feeling like you have to spend every waking moment on them. It's about being able to enjoy all facets of your life and not always having to be on. I highly recommend it.

I certainly picked and chose what was for me and what wasn't, but it has made my creative life a lot smoother. Pick and choose what works for you in this book—in any book. Take no one's word as gold. Learn to trust what works for you.

If any fear or anxiety seeps in when you want to begin your creative work, just start on it in spite of the fear. You're perfectly capable of creating some great work. Flip that fear around and sit down and start going over your work. I bet your natural instincts will kick in and you'll get some great work done.

When your mind wants to drift away and move on for the day. Do a little bit more work, just a tad. That will propel you forward the next day.

Start, and keep starting. The more you start on your creative work, the easier it will be to start. Just dedicate five solid minutes to your work. Then give yourself a reward after that. Then go up to ten minutes, then thirty minutes. Then give it a couple hours. Keep starting, and you'll begin wanting to start. You'll often be excited to start your day or your project. But only by starting consistently will you get to that point. Then the starting will almost start itself. So start on your creative work the next chance you get. Perhaps that's this very moment. If any fear or blocks remain, choose to start anyway. Move through the fear and those blocks will begin dissolving.

Overcoming Procrastination

Procrastination feels like this unsurpassable mountain that's always standing in the way of starting work on your projects. It feels like you have to scale a peak each time you begin. But that's only your mind standing in your way, only thoughts.

What if, instead of allowing those thoughts to stand in your way and create obstacles, at the very first thought of procrastination, the very moment you notice the obstacle, you go beyond it and just begin.

Simply start working on your project at that very first obstacle the mind wants to toss in your way. Use the obstacle as a jumping off point. Just begin, and the flow will sweep all of the obstacles away. Keep starting. Then, those mountains will level out. The flow will wash them away. Then you're just left with yourself and your creativity, your flow. Don't even think about working or creating, simply start going over your project and the starting will take care of itself.

Simply recognize the mind putting these obstacles in your way. Then you can go beyond them at any moment. You can go beyond mind's distracting thoughts and just start on your work. If any thought about your project pops up, run with it. Even if it's a thought about why you don't want to start, train yourself at that very moment, to start anyway. Choose to begin then and there.

Choose to start. Continue to start. The more you start, the closer you'll be to finishing. Don't look at the finish line and think, "I have to get there, but it's so far away." Instead, think of when and where you can start next. Let the flow wash away any obstacle.

This is what you love. Of course you're going to make time for it. You don't have to be overflowing with ideas to sit down and get to work. You just have to sit down and start. Type one sentence, paint one stroke; one line; one chord progression…

Starting is the hard part. If you can simply start one tiny bit of your project, you will naturally continue on. Once you start, it's easy. Starting is where most of us have problems.

Start enticing yourself. Stop forcing yourself. Build a reward system. Start your work—reward yourself—start again. Reward yourself with something fun or a nice dinner or a pizza, or whatever. Start again. Reward yourself again. Then sooner or later, the work itself will be fulfilling enough to entice you.

You'll no longer need to reward yourself, but you'll get to reward yourself. Then it becomes doubly rewarding. The work is totally rewarding and fulfilling. Then you reward yourself? Now I bet that's something you could be into. I think anyone could. And I think you deserve it. My reward for finishing this book was a new pair of shoes. It wasn't much, but it still kind of excited me, and I'm a dude.

Stop fighting yourself and forcing yourself. Start enticing and rewarding yourself. Simply start and simply flow. The more you're in the flow, the more you'll want to be, and the easier it will be to start flowing. Simply hop into the river. Let it flow.

Flow for a while, then climb out and dry off for a bit. Then hop back in. Eat some food. Go for a walk. Swim. Nap in a hammock. Enjoy the art, the flow. And enjoy being out of it. Get some rest. The creative flow doesn't have to be constant, and it won't be. And thank goodness. It shouldn't be. That would be exhausting.

For myself, it used to be challenging to start something and continue it for even an hour. Now I tend to write for several hours a day, five days a week. Though I am quite frequent in my breaks. There's not much I love more than taking a five to sit on the patio at a co-working space or coffee shop, or perhaps taking a stroll down the sidewalk. Start. Flow. Take a break. Start again.

Get up and walk around every hour or two. Taking small five minute breaks throughout the day will really help keep you fresh and in the flow. Take your break. Then begin again. Breathe. Flow. Ebb and flow.

Instead of picking up your phone and checking social media, check in with your mind. Sit with your mind for a minute or two. It doesn't need to be any longer than that. These aren't hour-long meditations. The methods are simply to make finding space easier, to make starting easier, and help you flow.

Breathe deeply. Find some space beyond your distracting thoughts—rest and breathe there for maybe thirty seconds, or five to ten breaths. Then hop into your work and begin. If you feel like picking up your phone, simply notice the urge, then come back to the breath. Breathe deeper and smoother, then hop back into the flow.

Also, quit always fighting the clock. Yes, get your stuff done and set goals. But on the day to day, if you're always trying to beat the clock, to get this or that done in a set amount of time, you'll likely exhaust yourself. That's quite un-zen. See if you can relax. It's not that serious. Wouldn't it be nice to not always be worrying about what time it is or how much work you can jam into this short little stretch of time, yet still getting all of your work done?

Once you stop fighting the clock, your life may just get much more relaxed and enjoyable. And I bet you'll get a lot more done. Plus, it will be better work, because you won't be rushing and fighting against time—you'll be flowing with it. So relax, do something you want to do instead of something you have to do. Then, choose to work on your project for any amount of time. Simply find some space—begin—and flow, as gently or energetically as the flow may be in this moment. Flow with it.

You can always use the blue sky method or some deep breathing to clear away any distracting thoughts that may be standing in your way and keeping you from starting your work. If you take a few deep full breaths and sit down with your project, I bet you'll catch the flow and get some great work done. Starting now is all it takes. Go for it.

Beyond Procrastination

Since your mind is what catches the flow, it may sound contradictory to go beyond thoughts or mind to get into the flow. However, the mind is often too cluttered with various thoughts to flow onto any one thing for long. Don't force thoughts to stop or try to throw them out. Just watch them. Forcing them to stop will also stop the flow. It will become a block, a dam, and the flow will be forced to stop.

What you can do, is find some space behind, beyond, or around thoughts. Just observe your thoughts. Feel the space around them. Be in the space. Breathe. Then hop into the flow, into the river, and go with it. Let it happen. It will. Even on days that you didn't plan to get any work done, you may decide to. Even days you feel off, take a little extra time, breathe a few extra breaths and deepen them.

Try stopping your breath all together and notice how thoughts stop. Find space behind and between thoughts. Then breathe deeply and watch the thoughts flow again. Be the space as they pass, the observer, rather than following every thought. Rest in the space. Then sit down with your work and begin.

Entice yourself. Build a reward system. Use a pull system instead of a push system. If, for a reward, you want to eat a pint of ice cream—do your work, then reward yourself. Good. Enjoy it. Or, if you want to play video games—start your work, then reward yourself with a game, fully able to enjoy it after having completed some work on your project.

You'll feel good about the work you've done, and you'll be able to truly enjoy your reward for once; and your free time; instead of feeling like you always have this cloud of work hanging over you. Allow yourself the freedom to actually enjoy your free time and your rewards. That's a lot easier to do after completing some daily creative goals. Accomplish a task, then reward yourself, truly allowing yourself to enjoy it.

Be kind to yourself. Entice yourself. Reward yourself for a period of work well done. Don't force it. Don't say you have to do this. You chose to do it, so do it in a relaxed way, in this moment—not in some other moment off in the future when everything's perfect and you're totally overflowing with ideas. Why not do it now? Find some space and let yourself flow. Then your project will stop feeling like this huge impossible task. It will start feeling like a perfectly possible series of small tasks.

You get large projects done by doing one little piece at a time. No large project is done in one sitting. You'll come back to it again and again, doing one small piece, then another. Then by and by, and possibly much sooner than you would have thought, the project will be done, and you'll feel a great accomplishment.

You don't have to get things done in perfect order, or exactly how you planned. When flowing, you're free to skip around as you please, knowing you'll be able to come back and flow into any skipped parts, finding new and interesting ways to connect the parts.

Don't have what you need to begin? Use what you do have. At the very least, you can always do a little planning or development, instead of waiting for the perfect moment. The perfect moment will never come. Only after you start and keep starting will you have those perfectly fulfilling creative moments.

The more you start, the more desensitized you'll be to any fear of starting you have or any procrastination. No fear of starting, of finishing, or ability will be able to get in your way. You'll simply begin. You'll take a couple of full deep breaths and flow into your work. No pressure, just release.

Your creativity and flow will become a place you can release any pressure you have from other aspects of your life. And your creative flow will flow into other parts of your life. You'll feel more confident and decisive. You'll see solutions to problems. Instead of being focused on the problem, you'll start focusing on the solutions. You'll be able to find the problems, the blocks, and the flow will wash them away. Finding space and observing the blocks will wash them away. Then, jump into your creative project and flow. Then no block or problem can stand in your way. Solutions to any problem will flow. Your projects will come to life.

Simply find some space, get back to that blank slate, and flow. Breathe and flow. The breath is far more important to our state of mind than we often realize. A few full deep breaths can really renew your focus and bring you back into the moment.

Rewards and Goal Setting

Don't force yourself, entice yourself. Build a reward system that pulls you towards starting on your projects and pulls you towards your goals, large and small. Don't push yourself to begin your work, or try to push yourself past your goals. Don't shove yourself.

Work with your mind, not against it. If you have rewards laid out along your project's journey, your mind will naturally want to reach the goals. You'll be working with your mind.

This book has mentioned setting goals and rewarding yourself when you reach them. This chapter will give you some ideas on how to build a reward system which will entice you to reach your goals and complete your projects.

Having a reward system will also help if you ever experience a lack of inspiration or you're feeling discouraged for any reason. It will help you start on your projects daily and follow through with them until the end.

The rewards for reaching your daily, weekly, and long term goals can be anything you like—as free, cheap, or expensive as you want—and as reasonable—don't go into debt to reward yourself.

Set rewards that entice you. Here are some simple examples: chocolate, a drink, a meal out, a friend hang, TV time, a concert, a night out on the town, a toke, camping trip, day hike, new shoes/suit/dress/gadget/bag/accessory, massage, yoga class, pizza, ice cream, time to meditate, a bath.

Your rewards can be literally anything. Just make them entice you. That's all that matters. Have rewards laid out that make you excited to begin your day and reach your creative goals. Once you reach your daily goal, you get to reward yourself—then the next day, and the next. Then before you know it, your project is done, and you get to enjoy your long term reward. Then you get to start a new project with new enticing rewards, or you can take some time off as a reward.

Set short and long term rewards for goals you reach. Feel free to set daily goals, weekly goals, and monthly goals. However, don't be extremely strict about them, or make them overly difficult.

In fact, make your daily goals easy to reach at first, where you easily blow past them. Feel how good it feels to accomplish all of your creative goals of the day, the week, and the month. You'll likely get much further along than if you set difficult to reach goals.

It's almost reverse psychology, where you're saying you barely have to try, then you may end up going above and beyond. Rather than laying out this long and difficult goal, set easy to reach goals. Don't set daily goals that you're only capable of reaching on the days you're overflowing. That will make you feel down on a gently flowing day.

At first, set goals that you can reach on a very gently flowing day. Then, after you continue to easily surpass your daily goals for a few weeks, perhaps set your goals a little higher, but not by much.

Then when you're very used to flowing past your goals, set goals that you can reach on a normal day, which you'll still blow past on days you're overflowing. But yes, on the really gentle flowing days, you may miss the daily goal. But that won't matter, because you'll offset the gently flowing days with the good-flowing and overflowing days, so you'll still be reaching your weekly goals and long term goals.

By setting easy to reach goals, you'll be making your creativity, and starting on your projects, a positive habit—versus one you naturally resist and procrastinate on due to the force and stress you put on yourself when you set difficult to reach ones.

You'll be enticed to set harder and more difficult goals. But then it's harder to reach them. Therefore they become discouraging, because it begins to make you want to force to reach that goal.

The thing of it is, is that you're much likelier to get more done when you set easier to reach goals, because you're allowing yourself space to get it done. You're not forcing yourself to rush—the walls aren't closing in—you're allowing yourself space to flow. If there's no worry about accomplishing your daily goal, there will be much less anxiety towards starting. Then the finishing will take care of itself.

Aim for a good middle ground, where yes, you set solid goals to accomplish your projects. Yet they're not difficult enough that you struggle to reach them. By starting with simple daily goals, you're likelier to reach your loftier and more long term goals with much greater ease and far less stress.

Daily goals can be anywhere from working on your project for thirty minutes, up to four hours, or as long as you'd like. Or, you can set your daily goals by the amount of work you accomplish, which is usually what I do. Starting out, simply having a reward for a solid thirty minutes of work is a great motivator. Then have another reward for the next thirty minutes of work, then move onto an hour, then perhaps two.

Then at a point, maybe you'll want to switch over to setting goals by the amount of work you accomplish, totally forgetting the clock, while still making the goals easy to reach.

For weekly goals, it's also nice to set easy to reach ones, basing them off your daily goals. And if you zoom past your daily goals one week, perhaps you'll wind up a whole day ahead of your weekly goal.

Once you begin easily surpassing your daily and weekly goals on a regular basis, perhaps increase your goals by just a touch—not enough to give any hint of discouragement—just enough to feel a slight growth.

At some point, you'll reach a nice middle ground with your goals. They won't be difficult to reach, but they don't feel too easy. Where you're able to flow without force, while knowing that you'll be reaching your goals and finishing your project in a timely manner.

With writing, I like to reward myself for each completed draft, with the best rewards laid out for the first and final drafts. I believe I wanted to have the first draft of this book done in six weeks, but I completed it in five. I kept wanting to force myself to get it done in four, but this was really not the book to force, so I allowed myself to relax by setting easier to reach goals. I didn't have to struggle to reach my daily or weekly goals like I would have if I tried to force myself to finish quicker.

I didn't set my daily goals up near the maximum amount of work I can do in a day. I set them at a middle ground, and I reached somewhere between them. I didn't pass my daily goals every day for this book, but I did pass my weekly goals and the overall goal of finishing the book within six weeks. If I really tried to force myself to finish in four weeks, I would have stressed myself out, and it would have most likely taken longer. Plus, I would have likely ended up having to do a lot more rewriting to make the book flow.

For setting and reaching long term goals (be it writing a book, an album; editing, producing or acting in a film;

painting a series, designing a home, or even starting a company) the most important thing is starting daily, or whenever you have time set aside for your projects.

Reaching your daily and weekly goals is what's going to allow you to reach your long term goals. You'll begin to flow to and through your goals with a much greater ease.

Have a nice reward laid out for reaching your long term goal. It doesn't need to be expensive or cost anything. Maybe have a small party with your favorite people or go camping for a weekend. Just make your long term goals things that excite you. Maybe there's a concert or festival you really want to go to.

Follow through with your daily and weekly goals, then your long term goals and projects will take care of themselves.

I tend to only put goals on one project at a time, then any work done on other projects is a bonus, making that project easier to finish when it becomes my main focus. More than that, and it could get messy for myself. But if you're juggling multiple projects at once, simply set goals for each. And if you're part of a team, set rewards for the team, such as a pizza lunch, a game afternoon, or a long weekend if they blow past the goal early.

Set reasonable goals as a team, then reward the team after reaching them. With reasonable goals, the team will be likelier to blow past the goals with much less stress while having a much better time. They'll flow through and past the project rather than forcing and stressing about it the entire time.

That's how you can create a thriving team environment. If you must set a stressful goal, make the reward that much more enticing. It doesn't have to be anything big, expensive, or time consuming, just something which will entice them. You don't even have to tell them, nor do you always have to give them a reward. Perhaps just use rewards sporadically. Though I bet the team will be more productive if there's a reward at the end of the tunnel. That's just human nature.

Use your human nature to your advantage—lay out some rewards this week for goals you complete—which you will complete.

Beyond Perfectionism

Perfectionism is the ultimate judgement. "Everything must be perfect; no dull spot; perfect shine; no dirt; no edge; everything in its perfect place; no coloring outside the lines; this way and nothing else will do…"

Screw all that noise. It's nearly impossible to flow if you're being such a perfectionist during the creative process. If you're an engineer, do product design or something similar, sure, you probably need perfect measurements—but not in most creative endeavors, nor while you're in the creative process. At the very least, try to save your perfectionist tendencies for the editing stages.

To truly flow, you're going to have to learn that horrible/amazing feeling of vulnerability, of the unknown. You're going to have to learn to allow it to exist. Otherwise, if you're practicing perfectionism, it will be a horribly painful chore to ever get close to finishing anything. If you do complete your project, it could still end up good, maybe even great, but getting there won't be very enjoyable.

Having to have everything perfect all the time? That sounds like creative hell, especially while you're there trying to create in the moment. How can you create if you expect every word, line, brushstroke, or chord to be perfect? I'm not sure, but it'd be tough, and you'll probably end up with an indention in your desk from banging your head against it so hard.

How can you get over perfectionism? Simply watch, and feel. Feel the discomfort. Feel the fear of imperfection. Why is it there? Are you afraid others will judge you? Some people will, no matter how perfect your project is. Quit giving them the power. The power is yours. Don't fear uncertainty. Don't fear failure. If you do fear failure, just allow it to be there. Feel it. Watch it. Watch your thoughts and judgements about your imperfection. Then find the space between/behind/around those thoughts.

Be the sky. Watch the clouds. Don't attach to them. Feel any nervousness. Breathe. Breathe deeper. Breathe into any fear, into the uncertainty. What's the worst that could happen? Someone doesn't like your work? So what? They probably wouldn't like it if it were amazing, because we all have different tastes. A lot of stuff people really love makes me cringe.

A note isn't perfect? The right word just won't come? The color or definition is not exactly how you want it? So what? Learn to live with that. Flow through the imperfection. Don't force yourself around it. Flow with new ideas on how to improve it. Don't stop and worry. Get your worrying mind out of it, and see what happens. Just go for it. Create.

Later on, sure, go back to rewrite and polish your work. But if you're expecting everything to be perfect from the get-go, you'll just be stuck in perpetual procrastination. Instead, learn to be in perpetual flow—or simply how to get your flow back. Your work will continuously get better and better on its own, without force or stress. Take it easy on yourself. You're improving your craft every time you work and flow on your creative projects. If anything's not working, you'll find creative solutions to improve or change it.

Learn to flow, and you'll love your art, your creativity. It will be alive. It will flow. It will fulfill you. Don't let a little fear of uncertainty or self-judgement get in your way. One day you'll get to where you want to be creatively, simply by flowing, by creating.

If you're practicing perfectionism, you'll be very likely to procrastinate, you'll struggle, and it may even seem painful. Your creative work will most likely not be an enjoyable experience, when it should be. Move beyond perfectionism. Do that by accepting the uncertainty and the fear of imperfection. Feel it. Breathe into it. Don't allow it to control you. It's blocking you. It's blocking your flow, and keeping you from being anything but perfect.

The only real way to get anywhere close to perfect is to flow every time you work on a project. Then go back and edit it, while flowing. Then rewrite it again, while flowing. Do that until you're happy with it. Don't expect perfection from the get-go, because there is no way it will come, no matter how much of a genius you are or how forceful you are with yourself. Accept that. Accept imperfection. Accept yourself, and grow from there.

Force is your creative enemy. It will not help. It will only hinder. Feel the constraints perfectionism has put on you. Feel where it's kept you stuck, procrastinating day after day, minute after minute. See it for what it is—a fear of the unknown, a fear of judgement, a fear of imperfection—a block of flow.

Learn to make your mind your friend, not your enemy. Accept it. Accept where you are. Accept imperfection. You want to flow, yes? Then stop judging yourself and expecting perfection. Accept that the more you allow yourself to flow, the more you'll continuously be improving—because you will—that's just how it works.

You'll look back at creative work you did a few years ago, that you thought was amazing (and may very well be), and see how much further along you've come. Because the more you flow, the more you'll improve. It's just nature. That's how we work. That's how the flow works. Allow it to work. Flow with it. Let the space be there. Breathe. Breathe deeper, smoother, and flow.

Don't Wait For Inspiration

If you only create when you're feeling fully inspired, then you're missing out on a huge portion of your creativity. Plus, you're missing out on a lot of inspiration. The more often you create and flow, the more inspiration will come. You'll start feeling fully inspired to begin your days. But you're not going to get there by waiting for inspiration to show up on its own. Keep starting on your projects, and the starting will be easier. You'll flow, and the inspiration will come.

Waiting for inspiration to strike is almost a fear. Why can't you create when you're not overflowing with inspiration? That overflowing inspiration is the same as when the flow is overflowing, and that doesn't happen all of the time. And I'm glad. That would be exhausting. Learn to cultivate your own inspiration. Waiting on it makes you almost a beggar. "Please come, inspiration. What will I ever do without you? I need you. Please."

Don't wait, cultivate.

Cultivate inspiration by starting, by choosing to devote time to your creative projects. Mend the soil—plant the seeds—water the soil. Get your left and right brain working together. Develop the idea and plan, then put that plan into action—be it an outline, a treatment, notes, a progression or a lick, a sketch—go for it. Quit waiting for inspiration. Start. Keep starting. And inspiration will find you.

Yes, every once in a while, you will have those random inspirational overflowing waves. Ride them. Flow with them. Once it's gone—fine—accept it. Then start your creative work anyway. Keep starting, and you'll start enjoying the gentle flowing days almost as much as the typhoon days.

Enjoy the calmness. Enjoy the rapids. Both are fine. Flow with both. Start, keep starting, and inspiration will flow.

If this book inspires you to create, use it. If other books or audiobooks do, use them. Listen to music that inspires and moves you. Listen to some orchestral music, such as Stravinsky or Ravel. Use a method. Start and keep starting.

The more you start working on your creative projects, the more inspiration will find you. Instead of being in a procrastination loop, you'll begin to get into a creative, productive, and inspirational loop.

The Space

Notice the space around you—the air, the sky—the space between the atoms and electrons. It's what allows life to live, to breath. There is so much space. Yet, we like to believe otherwise, especially in ourselves and the world. But really, matter is what? Basically nothing. Just atoms hanging out, rotating and spinning together in harmony. They're able to do this because of all the space.

No space, no life. The space is where life grows, where creativity grows and flows through. Creativity is life. Life is creative. It doesn't matter whether you believe in creation or a creator, you can still recognize how creative this life is and can be. Sure, there's a lot of monotony, but remember what it was like as a kid and those moments where everything was flowing.

Look at all of the creativity and inventions of the last century or so alone—electricity, computers, phones—films and music. Look at all the genres of music created in the past century and all the great artists, songs, and styles. That's a lot of creativity in such a short period of time.

Of coarse life is creative. So create. Stop delaying and get to it. Sit down with your work and begin. Create. Find fulfillment in creation itself. It's there. Let it flow. Find the space and allow the flow to happen. The space allows the flow. Allow the space to be, then begin and flow.

Even if your mind is totally full of thoughts and you think there is no way out, there is. The space is there. You just have to find it. Your mind needs space to concentrate and flow. Find space around your constant distracting thoughts.

If too many thoughts are clouding your mind, do a method. Find the space around and between thoughts. Simply watch. Be the space between the thoughts. Allow thoughts to pass. Be the vast clear blue sky.

If the space thing seems silly to you. Just take some deep smooth breaths and begin your work. Say "screw it," and just start. On an average day, I don't think about space at all. I'll typically just begin, or do a little breathing or stretching. However, finding some space can make it much easier to concentrate on and begin your creative work.

The space is always there to be found. The flow is always there to be accessed. All you have to do is find some space, or simply take a few deep smooth breaths. If all else fails, stop your breath for fifteen seconds and watch as you're tossed into the space between thoughts. Then begin your creative work.

Just begin. Start on one little piece.

And… go… now… yes… stop reading… set it down… set it down… And begin.

Go.

Start and flow. Breathe and flow.

102

Once you complete some solid work on a project, take a short break, then flow a little more, even if your mind's ready to give up for the day. Just do one more little task. That one little step might just propel you forward.

Space Grows More Spacious

Allow the space to grow more spacious. Don't force it. Don't pressure it. Let it happen. Give it the freedom to grow more spacious—simply by being with it—breathing into it —feeling—watching.

That will make it much easier to hop right into the flow. It will simply become easier to access. You'll just start flowing. Just by reading this, I bet you're getting new ideas about where your story could go, color palettes to use, or anything. Just reading this can help you find the space, or kick start you into wanting to begin working on your project. Simply breathing could get you back to that blank slate where you're ready to begin.

Breathe into the space—slowly—breathing in fully—filling your lungs entirely.

If you don't care for the space analogy, just breathe. Breathe fuller and deeper than you may ever have.

Empty every drop of air from your lungs—every single drop —slowly.

Continue breathing—deeper and fuller—filling and emptying your lungs totally—ebb and flow.

Feel the space. Just feel. Feel your hands. Feel the air. Feel your jaw relax, your shoulders drop. Breathe. Just be with the space. Your jaw relaxes more, and your feet. Feel. Watch as the space become more spacious.

The space is infinitely spacious. Allow it to be. Breathe into it. Breathe naturally… observe…

Now jump into the river, or straight into the ocean, and start on any aspect of your project, large or small—simply begin.

If distracting thoughts are holding you back from starting—keep breathing. Follow your breath instead of following your thoughts. Follow the breath in as your belly, ribs, chest and back expand. Continue following the breath as it flows out, and your belly, chest, back and ribs compress. Stay with the breath. When distracting thoughts pop up, go back to your breath and continue following it—in and out—ebbing and flowing.

Now, go to your workstation, while continuing to follow your breath. Continue following your breath as you begin going over your project. You'll naturally be inspired to start your work as your mind kickstarts into action and begins flowing with ideas and creative solutions.

Overflowing

If you're overflowing on a project, just go with it. Sometimes your creativity will be overflowing and ideas come rushing out. There's really nothing else to do. There's no stopping you.

Enjoy the overflowing—live it—breathe it—flow with creativity.

When you're overflowing with creative ideas, capture as much of it as you can—record it—write it down—draw or paint it.

In this state, nothing is stopping you. Let it happen. When you're overflowing on a new idea, write it down or record it. Don't force memory. Get down enough to recall the idea later. You'll naturally begin knowing where you want your ideas to go and how best to accomplish that aim.

Simply capture as much of that initial inspiration as you can. Then later, you can come back and expand upon those ideas and themes. Don't think that you must complete the work or idea perfectly right then and there. Just flow with it.

You can't force an overflowing state. It just happens. It only comes around once in a while and can last for several minutes, a couple hours, to perhaps a few days or even weeks.

Overflowing is a state that comes only when you're ready for it. It happens without any trying or searching. It's not something you can bring about. However, coming back to that blank slate, where you're the clear blue sky and thoughts are clouds passing by, could certainly make the possibility more likely.

If the flow is slow, allow it to be slow. Just go with it. If there's a good flow, go with it. If you're totally overflowing, go with it. Different days, different moments, will have different flows. Jump into your work and see what happens. You may surprise yourself and get a whole lot accomplished. You'll only find out by starting your creative work. Then when your mind's ready to stray, create a little more.

Don't try to force overflowing. It can't be forced. It just happens. When you are overflowing, there's nothing to stop you. It's difficult for your mind to even distract you in this state. This state is totally unstoppable. Let it rage.

Enjoy the overflowing for as long as it lasts. Once it's gone, enjoy the easy flow. There won't always be an overflowing, but once you sit down with your work, some sort of flow will come. The overflowing is amazing, but if you were always overflowing, you'd never be able to stop it. And that could get messy. You can always flow, but it won't be an unstoppable river at all times. When you want to flow with your work, you can. When you want to flow with life itself, you can. When you just want to rest, you can.

If you were currently in an overflowing state, you wouldn't be reading this book. So once you finish this chapter, get started on your work and let the flow hit you however it may.

When I wrote this chapter, I was flowing slowly. Earlier that week, I was overflowing, and I could hardly sleep. It wouldn't be healthy to be overflowing at all times. How could you rest with so many ideas hopping around your head?

Some of the best creative days are when you can just sit down with your work and begin, and you flow. Maybe it will take a couple minutes to really get into it, but if you give it a little time and maybe a few deep breaths, the flow will come. Again, you're not forcing the flow, you're welcoming it—just by sitting down with your work and looking over it. Simply begin and you'll begin flowing.

If you're not flowing how you'd like, maybe you need to lay out some structure and foundation with your left brain. Or perhaps you're ready to flow with your right brain. It doesn't matter, start and the flow will happen. Let the methods go, and just start. Be with your work. The flow will come, perhaps immediately, maybe after a few minutes, maybe after five or so. If you follow your inhale and exhale for several deep breaths, I bet you'll begin flowing right when you begin your work.

When you're overflowing, the flow is unstoppable, and there's really nothing you can do—so flow with it—no need to think about anything—just flow.

Know that the more consistently you start working on your creative projects, the more likely you are to have those unstoppable flowing moments and days.

When The Flow Is Slow

Perhaps things seem to be moving slow, you're not very into your work, new ideas just aren't coming or they're not going anywhere. The day I wrote this, that's how it was for me.

So, what can you do to get into a better flow? Breathe. Deepen, lengthen, and smooth out your breath.

Allow your body to relax as you breathe deeply. Find some space, or your center, and breathe into it.

Let the flow be slow. Don't try to force it to be quicker. If you are, simply notice.

Maybe this is the exact pace you need right now. Or perhaps you need to use your left brain to do a little organizing—flow into it. Don't give up on your work just because you're not overflowing. You can accomplish a lot even when your creativity is flowing slowly.

Or, maybe you need a break. If that's how it feels, take a break. Relax. Walk. Do anything you want—a handstand. Go out on the town or to a yoga class. Sleep. Watch TV. Listen to music—whatever—waste time. Don't judge yourself if you want to waste time. Accept it.

However, if you want to flow into your work, find some space beyond thoughts. Find your center, if you're into that sort of thing. Be with the space, with your center, with whatever you choose to call it. Or simply breathe deeply.

Find the space. Be the clear blue sky. Watch thoughts pass by. Breathe into the space—slowly—deeply—smoothly…

Now begin. Start with a simple tap on the keyboard, fret or drum—unscrew the paint cap, get out your brushes—open up your laptop, read where you left off, type one word—simply take one tiny step towards starting on your project.

Once you do that little tiny thing to start, your natural creative and problem solving instincts will kick in and you'll get into the flow—no matter how slow or quick it may be. Just do that one little thing to get moving—right now.

Flowing When It's Not Flowing

Have you not been feeling very creative or focused lately, or simply today? Don't be discouraged when you can't seem to flow or focus on your project. Perhaps some distracting thoughts are standing in the way of your flow, or maybe it's something deeper.

Even if something is bothering you and weighing on you heavily, you can still access flow and get some quality work done. If other things are bringing you down or worrying you, you can still flow.

You can flow no matter what's going on in your life or the world. Plus, it may help you cope. If you have a little time to work on your project, try to see if you can flow with it. You may even see it in a new light, which could be good for the project.

Trying to drown out something that's bothering you won't really help, and could create another block, a pretty deep block. Maybe you need to flow with what's bothering you into a creative pursuit. Getting it down in some creative form may help you move through it and free your flow. If you write something, say about a problem with your significant other, it may allow you to flow onto something you'd rather be working on. Perhaps getting the flow of something else out of your system will free your flow.

Even if you seem to be unable to flow in this moment, you can. Spend a little extra time with a method. Really breathe deeply. Focus only on the exhale and let the inhale take care of itself. Really focus. Follow the breath in and out.

Perhaps use the one-point focusing method, where you focus on one point and continuously refocus on it when your eyes or mind stray. It will help strengthen your focus and make it easier to concentrate on what you want.

Find what's blocking you. Simply watch, and you'll find the block. Keep watching it. Because by watching it—by feeling it fully and breathing into it—it will dissolve. Like darkness in the light, it will vanish.

Then you're once again left with a blank slate—the space for creativity to flow through. Find the space—that blank slate—take some full deep breaths and you'll start flowing again—almost like magic.

Or perhaps totally change it up. Get out and live some life. Go for a run or a hike—have a drink—do a hobby—play a sport or a game—whatever you like to do. Just stop trying to force the flow. Flip it and do something totally different than normal. Get out there and truly live. What's something you really enjoy doing—maybe something you haven't done in years? Try it. Then when you're ready, the next day perhaps, take some deep full breaths and begin. I bet you'll be able to flow right off the bat.

Find some space between your wandering thoughts. Don't force them away. Be the sky. Allow distracting thoughts to pass without clinging to them or giving them any attention. Breathe into the space, the sky. Allow it to become more spacious. Then simply begin—flow gently into your craft.

The more you begin, the more you create, the closer you'll be to completing your goals. You'll never know what could be if you simply sit back and think instead of taking action. You'll only truly know by doing, by starting, by creating. Perhaps there's something great inside of you that you'll only find when you truly begin giving it your all.

Flowing When Uninspired

How can you flow when you're uninspired, lacking confidence, or you're tired? Sleep could certainly help that last one. But you want to get something done now. You want to feel enthused and energetic, but you're not. So, how can you flow when you're uninspired or lacking energy?

When you're uninspired, learn to dive into your project anyway. Maybe it will take a moment to really catch the flow, or perhaps you start flowing the moment you sit down with your project. Some days you may need a method. Some days you'll be able to flow right off the bat.

See if you can start on your project and get any little amount of work done. Go with however mighty or gentle the flow is. Just start and see how it goes. Go to where you do you creative work and begin.

If you're tired, feel the tiredness. Don't fight it. Allow it to be there. Allow the tiredness to be heavy. Let your shoulders and limbs lay heavy. Let your energy melt into the ground. Don't force yourself to be wakeful. Feel your lack of energy. Don't fight it. Let it fall.

Let thoughts pass. Always following thoughts is tiring, so try not to latch onto them. Allow thoughts to drift away as you sit or lay heavy, like clouds in the sky. Instead of following your thoughts, follow your breath for several inhales and exhales.

The morning I wrote this part, I was a little sleepy and jumping into writing wasn't my first idea of a good time. Yet, I chose to. Yeah, I was a tired, but I was still able to do some good work.

You may need to use a method. If a method works, use it. If not, find something else to get into the flow, or simply do some deep breathing. You've just got to get over the resistance of starting. Because the more you start dipping your toes in, the easier it will be to dive in headfirst whenever you'd like.

Drink an extra cup of coffee or tea if you feel the urge. Or perhaps you may need to hydrate. Drink more water than you think you need. You'll be surprised by how much energy water itself can give you. It can also help clear away fogginess.

If you need to feel more awakened, instead of feeling heavy, imagine you are total lightness, that you're floating. Imagine you're lighter than a feather just floating in the air. Drift in the wind. No effort is needed to hold yourself up. You're simply breathing, floating—slow, gentle movements—flowing with the breeze.

No holding onto anything—just releasing—floating—drifting. Relaxing totally with zero effort—gently—slowly—breathing—floating. Your face relaxes, your eyes, your cheeks, your jaw, neck and shoulders

Now start your project. Let your flow be slow if that's how it's flowing. That's how I was flowing—barely at all. But this lightening, floating method made me feel much better and lighter about the whole day. It sort of opens the entire body to flow and can really lighten the load.

Perhaps go for a walk while doing this method. Allow yourself to be light, letting yourself flow freely. Then, you can come back to your work with a bit of freshness. Still perhaps flowing very gently, but flowing nonetheless.

Allow the flow, don't force it just because you feel you need to get something done. Choose to get something done, then reward yourself with something small that you enjoy after you meet your day's goal. You'll naturally move towards your goal if you reward yourself for work you complete.

I felt like rewarding myself more than usual the week this was written. Usually the work is fulfilling enough, but sometimes that extra enticement of a reward will be that extra boost you need to get moving on your project. You don't even have to know what the reward will be. Just knowing that you'll reward yourself will be enough. It will make it easier to simply sit down and begin your creative work.

Notice when your mind wants to drift off. Just observe it. Don't judge it. Judging the mind will make it run further. Accept it. Watch it. Then focus back on the task at hand—roll with it—hop in and begin. If the flow's slow, it's slow. Let it be. Flow gently into your project.

Perhaps you're not flowing because you're lacking confidence, which is making you feel uninspired. Where has the confidence gone that you had when you began the project, had the original idea, or when you were really flowing?

Why can't you still feel that confidence? Feel the lack of confidence. Feel why you may be lacking confidence. Watch it. Watch your mind—how it clings to these thoughts of insecurity. Breathe into the thoughts. Find the space behind those thoughts. Breathe into the space.

Thoughts are nothing but a smokescreen, clouding the space and blocking your flow. There is zero insecurity when you're flowing—you're too busy creating. You're perfectly capable of creating something great, and finishing long, difficult projects. You'll get the confidence back. You'll get it back by beginning on your projects and flowing. Jump in, take a few full deep breaths, and flow.

As you continue to flow, your skills will continue to grow in depth. You'll start creating things that you're excited about —beyond what you previously thought you could ever do. No matter if you're anywhere near where you want to be creatively or not, I have confidence that you will get there if you continue starting and flowing.

Breathe and flow.

Get a little zen and create.

Repetitive Works

How can you flow if you often have to do repetitive, mundane work? Perhaps you're tired of playing the same old songs, or designing the same kind of art, working on the same projects, editing the same show or type of video or music, or teaching the same material? How do you flow if you're just doing the same thing over and over? How do you flow when you're doing almost mechanical creative work or performing?

Don't get stuck on thoughts about how tired you are of this work, or why you can't do this other thing you'd rather be doing. Watch those thoughts. Why did you want to do this in the first place? And why has it merely become a chore rather than a joy? You don't necessarily have to quit or change careers. But you should try to find a way to make your work flow again. Go beyond thoughts, harmful or helpful. Find space and try to really come at the project from a blank slate.

Or try putting your creativity into another project. That could work wonders on your enthusiasm—no matter how large or small the new project, or if it's in the same field or something completely different and off the wall.

If you find new enthusiasm in something else, you can bring some of that back into your mundane work. You may end up being happy about not having to spend so much creative energy on it, leaving more for your passion projects.

Starting a new hobby or renewing an old one could also be very beneficial. Live your life outside of your work. Don't make your creative work your entire life. Play in a recreational sports league—have a game night—anything.

And exercise, of course—at least a little bit. It's incredible how much more energy you have for pretty much everything when you exercise regularly.

Find the blocks inside yourself. Find the thoughts holding you back. Watch the nagging thoughts about why you dislike what you're working on so much.

Perhaps you still enjoy what you're doing, but your mind's just going against you. Be the space behind your thoughts and watch them. Let those thoughts dissolve in the spaciousness.

If you can learn to flow anew into your work, you'll likely end up starting to enjoy it again. You've probably just let it become a nagging task, rather than a flow. It has likely became a place where pressure grows instead of releases. Make it a release again. Drop the forcing, the frustration, and flow.

We're so good at seeing the negative in things, in people, and in ourselves, that we forget things are usually pretty perfectly well and fine at most any given moment of everyday life. Do you have to be doing this work or project?

Not at all. But you chose to, so choose to give it your all. Choose to start. Choose to finish. Stop telling yourself that you have to do it. You don't. You can quit now. Though that probably wouldn't feel that great. Finish the project by continuing to start on it, then move on to something else if you choose.

Or realize that your work or project isn't so bad. Find space and bring some freshness back into your work. Allow the flow to spring and flow through the space. Feel the space. Let it be. Breathe several full deep breaths—in and out. Then sit down and begin your work—flow with it.

Feel free to place some rewards on your path as you complete your repetitive or mundane work for some extra motivation.

No Creative Bones

Do you believe that you have no creative bones in your body? The truth is, that's just not true. You're simply blocked or you're too afraid to try. Maybe you were judged for something you tried to create when you were younger, or you just never felt you were any good at anything creative.

Not many people are great at anything when they just begin. Of course there will be a few naturals, where they can't help but create in a given medium, but not many. Nor are there many who can just pick up a new sport or hobby and be great from the get-go. Don't be discouraged because you're not great at the start. That's a good thing. You have room to grow, where you can surprise, and perhaps amaze yourself as your abilities grow and multiply while you flow into your projects.

You're likely not going to be great when you just begin creating in a new art form. That's fine. Accept it. I certainly wasn't a good writer or storyteller when I began. I was naturally athletic and math-oriented, and never read a book until I was eighteen. It took me at least five years to even begin understanding story. Now, many years later, I'm fully confident in my ideas and my ability to follow through with them and create a fun and compelling story.

That may sound like a long time, however when you really enjoy what you're doing and what you're creating, it doesn't feel like a long time. Sometimes it can be a bit of a struggle and can feel stressful. But when you learn to flow, that struggle and stress will drift away, and you'll just be in the moment with your project. You'll enjoy it. You'll flow. Even if you're not a master of your craft yet, you'll get there, and you'll enjoy the process.

If there's something you're passionate about, get out there and try it. Make it happen. Jump in and give it a go. Don't judge yourself or your abilities, or even your procrastination. Accept yourself exactly as and where you are. Enjoy creating. Even if you think that what you're creating is terrible, I bet that your next project, work, piece or song will be better than the last. And you'll start enjoying the process more and more as your talents grow. Use the methods to find space beyond thoughts. Then drop the method, start on your project fully-focused and flow.

You don't find the flow with the methods. The methods can only be used to find and create space—to get you back to that blank slate. Once you've found the space or the flow hits, drop the method and flow naturally. Focus only on the work at hand.

If distracting thoughts start popping up, simply notice, and choose to focus back onto your project. If you want to check something on your phone—notice the urge—feel that pestering urge—then concentrate back on your creative work and continue—flow. That urge will begin to diminish.

Keep starting. Create a reward system for any amount of work you do. Find a little space and flow—reward yourself—and begin again. Create, and keep creating.

Finding Enthusiasm

What can you do when you can't find any enthusiasm for your project? First thing, stop looking for enthusiasm—just watch—slow it down.

Don't judge your non-enthusiasm. Accept it. Breathe into it. Keep breathing into it. Feel your non-enthusiasm totally. You may even get a laugh out of it as you notice how stubborn and ridiculous your mind is being. Allow it to be. Feel every drop of your non-enthusiasm. Feel it totally.

Don't force enthusiasm. Simply accept that you're not enthused. Watch your thoughts—breathe—slowly and smoothly. Observe your mind's grasping, connecting, and jumping. Breathe into your thoughts. Find the space around and within thoughts.

Use a method or a few combined. Use your own. Work out. Walk. Run. Go for a swim. Listen to music.

Find enthusiasm in another aspect of your life. Go out and have some fun. Play a sport. Invite some friends over. Change locations for the day.

Maybe you're feeling impatient. "Just be patient." That's like telling someone to relax. And it's not going to help you be patient. The only real way to be patient is to stop trying to be patient and find some space.

Being impatient is simply being attached to your distracting thoughts and being unable to go beyond them. You're waiting for this to be over so you can do something else. It's like a block, and acts the same as a creative block. It's an attachment to thought, to mind.

"Be patient." No. Don't be patient. Find the space between thoughts—beyond mind—the blank slate. Feel the excitement, anxiety, or nervousness the impatience is causing.

Feel the impatience. Just feel it. Just watch it. Just be with it. Allow it to be there. Don't fight it off. Accept it. Feel it. Feel the connections. Feel how it kind of ties your mind down, like a chain that can't break. Just watch it. By watching it, the chain will dissolve. Don't force it, watch it.

Become the vast sky behind and around the passing clouds of impatient thoughts. Watch them, feel where they're stuck in your mind or your energy. Just breathe. Breathe deeply. Allow the thoughts to pass.

Watch. Feel. Breathe. Be the sky, the space, the ocean, as thoughts wash over you. Don't catch them. Don't hold onto them. When one thought passes, don't search for it, don't allow the traces of it to catch you. When it's gone, allow it to be gone, even if it felt important.

Trying to find a lost thought will only make it evade you, sort of like an eye thingy. You try to follow it, it evades. That's exactly how thoughts work. When they're gone, they are not going to be found, so quit trying to find them. Let them be gone. Don't let them go, just let them be gone. The difference being, that when you let them go, you're kind of forcing them to be gone. When you let them be gone, you're unattached to them, and you stop searching for them.

You can't force enthusiasm. But you can allow yourself to enjoy the act of creation and to also enjoy your free time. If you can keep starting and flowing on your projects, enthusiasm will start finding you.

Flowing Passionlessly

What if you're working on something that you're not at all passionate about? You can still find fulfillment through it if you can find a way to flow with it.

Something that can really help if you're not enthused about a project or job is using some of The Now Habit methods, such as saying, "I choose to do this," versus, "I have to do this." It helps take away the pressure and force. Build a reward system for this project or job. Make it new. Be creative with it. Build enticement. Use a method to go beyond mind, to get back to that blank slate, then flow into your work.

Pull yourself through the end goal with rewards laid out upon the path. Don't shove yourself towards your goal. If you do, the natural rebel inside you will protest and you'll procrastinate your heart out. Entice your natural rebel with rewards that you'll truly enjoy.

The more you start on a project, the quicker you'll be done with it. Instead of saying, "This will take forever, I hate this." Say, "I get to get this out of the way, then I'll be closer to where I want to be. Then I'll be free to do the things I want."

How much freedom will you have once the work, day, or project is complete? Maybe it will allow you to move onto other projects or jobs that you're more excited and passionate about. Or maybe there's a fun reward awaiting you after the day's or project's end. Plus, you'll have more time to hang out with friends and family.

If you don't see yourself ever being passionate about this project, job or position, and find it difficult to flow—and if it always hangs over you like a cloud—perhaps it is time to start looking at moving on to something you are passionate about—something you can more easily flow into. Or maybe there's something you can get paid to do that doesn't take as much of your creative energy so that you can flow easier and more often into the projects you are passionate about. Find what works best for you in your life.

Even if there was something that you used to absolutely love doing with all your heart, if you don't love it now, don't force yourself to continue it. Unless it's simply a project that you truly set out to finish, simply finish it and move on to something you do truly love and that you are passionate about.

Or perhaps you've simply lost the passion for your current work or project, but you do still love it, and you want to find that passion again. Then simply learn to flow into it. Quit forcing it. Find space, and find the flow. That's how you'll find the passion again—by allowing your creativity to flow —by going beyond mind and its nonstop thoughts and distractions, and doing your work.

You won't be forcing yourself to work on the project, you'll be enticing yourself with rewards. Maybe you'll find that there's one or several particular aspects of your creative work that you're really passionate about, while others, you aren't. Then perhaps you can start focusing more time on the aspects you enjoy, while delegating aspects which discourage you to others who enjoy them. Or perhaps use methods to get you through the discouraging aspects so you can move on to the aspects you enjoy.

Maybe you've lost the passion simply because you've been forcing, which has created a block that you just can't seem to get around, and you're finding it hard to begin each day. Find the space to clear those blocks away. Breathe into it. Find the space between and around thoughts. Breathe into the space. Keep breathing. Follow your breath as you inhale fully and continue following it as you exhale every drop of air. Rest in the space for a moment as you breathe deeply. Now, begin your work, and flow.

Perhaps inspiration and passion will begin to flow through you as you flow into your project and even when you're away from it. If you can get back to that blank slate—get a little zen—I bet it will.

Finding Your Passion

The more you get into the flow, the more you'll find where your passions truly lie. Try any creative outlet you're interested in—flow with it—no matter how terrible at it you may feel you are. If you enjoy it, enjoy it. If not, find something else and flow with it. You won't find your passions by thinking about them. You'll only find them by trying and doing, by flowing.

If you already know where your passion lies, you'll still continue pinpointing aspects that you'll want to dive deeper into. Your current passions will lead you toward new ones. Creating in one form could naturally lead to another.

If you're handling multiple parts a project or perhaps every part, maybe you'll find that there are aspects that you genuinely love and give you fulfillment, while other aspects frustrate you.

That's perfectly fine. You'll begin to really figure out where your passions do lie, and perhaps you'll meet others who are passionate about the aspects that frustrate you and vice versa. That's where some great partnerships can be formed. You'll each find more and more fulfillment because you'll each be focused on the aspects that you each enjoy and inspire you—look at Matt Stone and Trey Parker—Trey does all the work while Matt cracks wise.

For myself, I would have never known that I wanted to write books if I hadn't written screenplays for years and made a couple silly films. I began writing screenplays to act, then realized I'd rather direct, but ultimately found that writing was my favorite aspect of filmmaking.

You'll get good at what drives you, and you may find others who need you because the other aspects drive them. You'll be flowing—they'll be flowing—you'll never find that until you get out there and give it a go.

If you want to do the parts that frustrate you, learn to flow into them as well. Perhaps you need to flow with your left brain to tackle those aspects, which will free your right brain to flow into the aspects you do enjoy.

Regardless of any of this, get out there and create. And be honest with yourself about the things you find that you truly enjoy versus those which frustrate you. If there's something you want to try to create, go for it. If you want to write something, write it. Make music—art—a film. Get out there and go for it. You'll never know until you try. The more you create, the more you'll continue finding aspects that truly enliven your spirit.

You owe it to yourself. Go out there and make it happen—create. You're perfectly capable, and the more you do create, the better you will get, and the more enjoyment you'll get out of creating. You'll fine-tune your creativity and your craft just by getting into the flow and doing what you love. Then, each thing you create will feel new, and inspiration will flow. You may even find that aspects which once frustrated you, now enliven you, because you gained new skills and it has become easier to flow though those aspects.

Writer's block? Forget about it. You'll be too busy flowing. You'll be free—you are free—you just may not know that yet. Or maybe you do. But it's not something you know, it's something you feel. And when you feel it, nothing and no one can stop you. You become an unstoppable force. It may take years, it may take months, it may take a decade to get where you truly want to be. But you'll find some wonder along the journey.

One day, you'll find yourself where you wanted to be, and possibly far beyond. You'll simply be in the flow, just like you can be today. It's almost as if the flow keeps building. It starts as a little stream, then it becomes a tributary, then a river, then a mighty river, then it becomes the ocean itself. Then there's a never-ending flow. All you have to do is allow yourself to access it—to turn on the tap. You can access it now. You can do that by going beyond distracting thoughts, by finding the space and naturally flowing into your projects, one step through the next.

Take some deep breaths and watch the mind. Be in the space as thoughts pass. Then, by and by, the flow will come.

Simply find or create the space for the flow to find you—plant the seeds—mend the soil—take a few deep breaths. Your skills and passions will grow and develop roots that can't be dug up, which will continuously fuel the flow. If you're able to go beyond distracting thoughts, you'll have everything you could ever need in your creative arsenal at any given moment to focus on your project and flow.

Part Three

Keep On Flowing

__Idea Creation And Organization__

An idea will often come to you out of nowhere at any moment. Something sparks it, or it just hits you. If a great idea comes to you, try to get it down as soon as you can.

When an idea flows to you, jot it down, record it, or sketch it. You'll continuously get better at getting the gist of an idea down. You may even be able to complete a movie outline or song in ten minutes. You'll flow with it. Simply write down or record, paint, or design what you can of the idea. Let it flow. Then later, you'll be able to come back to it, fully develop it, and run with it.

You won't be starting from scratch each day on your projects. You'll be starting from where you left off. You'll flow from there and continue onward towards your goal of completing the project.

One simple way to create and develop ideas is to ask yourself, what would you most want to see, hear, or read? Then go about developing that. Ask questions about it—answer them—select your favorite answers and expand upon them. Then ask new questions. What are the conflicts? Find and develop the structure, the colors, differences in characters and contrasting elements.

How I often select or brainstorm a project is by asking myself: what would I most want to see or read? Or, what would this audience like to see or hear that also excites me? Another good one is, what specific knowledge do I have that hasn't been put together in this certain medium yet? That's why I wrote this book, as every book on creativity I've read bores me to tears. Plus, none I found have any actionable zen aspects, and strongly lack motivational elements.

As a creative, it's good to always have something to take notes with. The notes app in your phone is a good place to start, where you can organize them by folder or anyway you want.

If you don't write an idea down when it comes to you, it will likely be gone. You'll want to try to find it, you'll try to hold onto that thought. But if it's gone, it likely won't be coming back. You just have to let it be gone. Maybe it will come back to you, perhaps it won't. If that happens, one thing you can do is write down anything that could remind you of the idea later.

For staying organized with various projects, gadgets work great. Maybe you prefer paper. Fine, but it's going to take more work to stay organized. If you do use paper, I'd recommend having some way to keep notes separated for different projects and various aspects of each project. Perhaps, have a different notebook for every project.

Personally, gadgets are the way to go. They're quite nifty— kind of like the mind—extremely useful—but yes, they can be a constant distraction. If you're a songwriter, perhaps paper is the best, as you can write chords in more easily. However, once written, it's still a good idea to organize them on your computer or phone.

Learning to organize your ideas will change your creative life. If you have scattered papers and different projects buried amongst each other, you're going to have a difficult time ever completing a project. Because every time you want to work on your project, you'll have to dig through stacks of papers just to begin. Therefore, you'll have a much more difficult time starting.

If you have everything organized, you can find anything you want with a couple of clicks, and begin. You won't waste time or energy searching for your notes and outlines and what-have-yous. They'll simply be right where you need them when you need them. To be a prolific creative, and to flow, you need to have easy access to your creative tools.

Brainstorming is like dipping your bucket into the well. You're just grabbing ideas without any judgement. Some will be terrible, some will be mediocre or fairly good, while some will be great or amazing. Don't judge while brainstorming. Just let it happen. Save your judgements for afterwords, when you're selecting your favorite ideas.

After you're done brainstorming and you've answered some questions about them, go back with your left brain to find the ideas which are your favorite and work the best. Ask more questions with your left brain, then let your right brain answer them freely, without judgement. Your right brain will expand upon the ideas and add new ones.

Then once more, use your left brain to select your favorite and best answers. Once you get that ebb and flow, there will be no fight, there will be no struggle. There will only be flow—left brain structures—right brain fills in the blanks and runs with it. Once the structure is ready, the right brain is free to flow its way to a completed first draft.

There is an infinite amount of creativity that you can tap into at any moment, which I used to call the infinite well of creativity. To access it, all you've got to do is get back to that blank slate and ideas will start hopping out of the well. All you'll have to do is flow with them.

If your mind's not distracted by various thoughts, about what happened or could happen, ideas will flow to and through you. You become a portal for them to flow through. All you have to do is dip your bucket in whenever you choose and pull out an idea, or maybe an idea will just hop out to you. If you like it, write it down. If you don't care for it, let it go. Then get back to that blank slate to access the well of infinite creativity once more.

Ideas will flow through you, and you'll develop them with ease. Those ideas will turn into paragraphs, verses, backgrounds—into chapters, songs, foregrounds—then before long, they'll turn into Acts, rough drafts, and full songs.

Then, sooner than later, they'll turn into the whole—into an entire book, screenplay, album, painting, series, design, or project. It will just happen. You simply start, keep starting, keep flowing—and by and by your works will come together. Completed projects will start piling up. Your creations will start becoming true works of art. You may end up creating masterpieces without even trying—simply by flowing into your creative outlets.

However, if you ever try to create a masterpiece, if you force it, I can almost guarantee that you won't end up with anything nearing a masterpiece. It won't feel alive. How could it? Don't worry if your every work is not a masterpiece. They won't be. Some people will love what you create, some people won't. Who cares? You certainly shouldn't by now. You like it, or you found fulfillment through it, or at the very least, it helped you improve and grow your creative skillsets.

Go back and improve upon your ideas with a fresh outlook. Nothing's done all at once. Going back to edit something you've already created doesn't harm creativity in any way. It only improves upon it. You'll flow with the editing as well—your mind will naturally find and improve upon various parts and aspects.

Don't judge your work if you're not happy with it, simply make it better. Or make your next creative work better. For myself with writing, it takes until around the fourth draft before I'm happy with it. When, before I understood story or learned how to develop and outline a story, it would take closer to ten drafts to be somewhat happy with a script. And they still felt patched together rather than being one succinct story, because I didn't develop and outline them fully. Therefore, I had a lot more work to do in order to (try to) make the story work.

There can often be more depth to be added to projects or excess to be trimmed. Fine-tune your work. Simply keep getting back into the flow and it will almost edit and rewrite itself. You're simply there with it, seeing it with a fresh pair of eyes.

Find space between thoughts, beyond mind and get back to that blank slate—where life flows through you—where ideas spring and grow from. Your prior judgements will have dissolved so you can see the project freshly and your natural problem solving brain will be focused on any needed solutions.

You'll learn to know when your project is complete. Perhaps in a month or two, coming back to it could bring totally new eyes, and you'll notice a few things that can really improve and finalize it.

Or perhaps, the project is finished. Congratulations. Get it out there, or get it to someone who can. Then start the next. Feel the excitement from what you've just completed. Let that flow into your new project, let it build up. It will. Keep starting. Keep creating.

Once you start finishing projects, you'll become better at selecting the ideas you really want to see reach the finish line. You'll get better at developing them and following through with them until they're completed. You'll flow into and through them, and before you know it, that project will be done, and you'll be onto the next one.

The better you get at developing your ideas from the get-go, the easier it will be to know exactly where to go next—where this piece fits—what's needed to connect different pieces—whatever the project needs. Simply find some space, and the ideas will flow through you, and you'll know just how to develop them in your own creative way. You only finish by starting. So, find a little space, begin, and flow. Keep flowing. You'll start finding fulfillment daily by the creative work you complete. All it takes is starting today.

Flowing With Structure

After an idea comes to you and you flow with it in that initial moment, perhaps you'll sit down with the idea a few more times to develop it out further, asking questions about it, answering them, selecting your favorites and what works best for the idea, progression or story.

Once you have an idea down and somewhat developed, you'll probably want to sit down to structure and outline it.

When I first began writing, I never structured. I just totally let it go anywhere with no guide. I got some good humor out of it, but it was totally unstructured with no story, only scenes. After a rough draft was finished, trying to go back and rewrite was a grueling disaster. I had to try to forcefully add story where none existed and try to patch all of these random pieces together. It wasn't much fun.

Finally, after producing two feature films, I began to figure out story. I began to outline and structure. I would do these huge outlines, up to twenty pages, with a separate outline for each somewhat significant character. That worked great, and it really helped my stories come to life. But now, I use a mix of the two—structured and unstructured.

Now, I like to have a simple outline. Enough so that I can stay on track and complete the story, script, or book in an efficient manner. Not so much that it gets in the way of my freedom and lays out every single step. That way, my right brain has a basic direction to flow towards, yet it's not being overly steered or micro-managed. And if any more structure is needed to clear things up, I can go in with my left brain and structure it, then flow through and around that structure with my right brain.

I do usually have a full outline before I begin a writing project of any kind, however with this book, I gave myself a few weeks of total free-flowing. And it was going great, until I was like, "Dang, this is going to get ugly and confusing fast."

So I sat down and outlined the whole thing, which made the process much simpler. My left brain was no longer duking it out with my right brain. I wasn't having to search or dig for what was needed or figure out where things should go. I was free to flow into and around the structure my left brain laid out.

An outline, or any structure, is not concrete. I'm always changing plot where it wants or needs to be changed. At times, I'll add elements that end up changing the entire structure. Then I'll need to figure out how to remold the outline to fit where I want the story to go and what works best with the new story elements.

Allow the flow to take you in the best and most interesting direction. Then, readjust your structure as and if needed.

With music, you may find a new chord, progression, or lyric that totally opens the whole song up. Don't be afraid of letting your creation expand.

In the first draft of my first novel, I completely changed the climax, adding some major character and plot changes. Therefore, I had to rework everything that was to happen after, and a good bit leading up to that point. But it added much more depth. It wasn't as sunny of an ending, but it was what felt right for the story, so I ran with it.

Allow yourself that freedom. Allow your right brain the freedom which structure offers by taking the stress out of creating. When working in structure, you won't have to ever stop to brainstorm new ideas or figure out what to do or where to go next. It's already laid out. Yet, you have zero obligation of sticking to it. Structure is simply a guide. Allow your right brain the freedom to break structure any time you see fit. Though we often feel it restricts us, structure allows your natural rebel to flourish.

Rewriting

Rewriting is an integral part of creating. Nothing's going to come out perfect in one draft. That's simply not going to happen. There will be some great parts and aspects in a first draft (or demo/design), but also some parts and aspects that can be improved upon—new elements to be added—twists, hooks, dialog, chord changes, or subplots to give more depth, contrast, and character.

Rewriting is turning the first draft into your true vision for the project—from sketch, to finished painting—from good into great.

A first draft is a Whiskey Cola or Gin & Tonic. A final draft is a Gold Rush or French 75. It's refined, has character, and all parts work together bringing out the fullness and completeness of the project. It's not simply tossed together—it's finely crafted.

If you allow yourself to go back and rewrite your work, it will be much fuller and more balanced, it will flow better and will be improved all around. If you're a writer who doesn't rewrite, you're not living up to your full potential. Rewriting is simply reading your work and flowing with any edits you'd like to make, transitions you'd like to add, or anything you'd like changed.

It's not as big of a deal as you may believe. There's really no reason to stress about rewriting. Simply flow with it.

Begin reading or going over your work, and you'll automatically know what you'd like to improve and what you love as is.

If you don't like rewriting, perhaps think of it as improvising off of what you've already done, or as a reading for a film production.

Rewriting isn't only for writing. I'm merely using the term rewriting. It can mean reworking and improving upon any idea or design, film editing, mixing, or even songwriting. And you're not actually rewriting anything—just making improvements and adding depth.

Rewriting is not your enemy. Nor is rewriting an uncreative venture, as you may believe. Rewriting is an integral part of creating. If you're not rewriting, you're missing out on one of your most important creative tools.

Maybe you think someone else will come in later and rework your creation after it's sold, or a producer or editor will come along and know just the right thing to do. That's unlikely. Or perhaps you think your first draft is perfect. I don't doubt that it's good, I doubt that it's finished.

Another very important thing from The Now Habit (perhaps the most important for myself) is that it says Harvard Literature students are taken into the library during initiation to read first drafts of famous works from the greatest of the greats, to show how incomplete and imperfect even their first drafts were. What really made those works great was rewriting.

So much depth can be added during the rewriting process. The basic story is there in the first draft, perhaps perfectly structured. But once you go back and read through it, you will find so many places where something can be added to give the story or scene more meaning, depth, conflict, comedy, or whatever it needs. You can do this with music or design, or most anything. Go back to it and find where something could be tweaked or repositioned just so much to really make it pop.

Rewrite, yes. But also don't get stuck in the dozen rewrite trap. If you're going over ten rewrites, really much over five, you probably didn't structure or outline your story well enough before you began, so you're having to add story elements and constantly rearrange things. That's why outlining and developing your story and characters thoroughly before you begin writing can be so important. You won't have to stop and worry about where to go, nor will you have so many missing pieces to fill in during the rewriting stage. Outlining makes rewriting much easier, as everything's already in proper order. Then with rewriting, you're simply making it better, instead of having to rework the entire thing. You're simply enhancing it as you flow through it.

Rewriting songs can also be useful. The more you play a song and flow with it, the more you'll find parts or lines that can be improved. It won't harm your original idea, you'll be simply improving it—perhaps with a line that means more to you—or one that you won't mind singing ten years into the future.

Demoing can really help finalize your songs and get them to where you truly want them. You'll be hearing the song without playing it for the first time, which can allow you to hear all the different parts clearer and how it sounds as a whole.

Perhaps you'll find a better melody or a new chord that really brings more life into it. If it works, it works. Go with it. If it doesn't, don't worry about it. Perhaps the very original was the best. Magic can come in either stage. Just don't be afraid to experiment with rewriting. It will often add just what was needed, as you'll be able to see the song or work from a bigger picture.

If a part, lyric, lead line, or rhythm isn't doing what you want it to. Why stress? Simply figure out one or more things that could really enhance it. Or perhaps something just needs to be removed for a bar or two (drums, bass, etc.), then it will really hit when it comes back in. Would a tempo change make it more interesting? Try really slowing the bridge down or speeding up the final chorus—experiment freely.

You can rewrite nearly any creative work. Going back to it, you'll see different nuances that you didn't see before, and you'll be ready with new creative solutions. You'll flow with solutions to bring your works to life and make them whole. Rewriting will enhance your works. Yes, particularly with any kind of writing, but rewriting can enhance any creative endeavor.

Rewriting is about making your work's whole—completing them in the best way possible—expanding your original draft until it's truly what you want it to be. It's about not settling for mediocre. It's about making your works great. Rewriting is not about reaching perfection. It's about making each work its best in its own unique and perhaps perfectly imperfect way.

Finishing Projects

The only way to finish a project is to keep starting. That's all you can do. Instead of always looking towards the finish line, look at what you can do now to move the project along. What's one little piece you can do now? If you're writing a book, an album, painting a series, editing a movie, writing a thesis or whatever, simply keep starting. Do small increments of work that lead to longer increments, then by and by, inch by inch, you'll reach your goal.

Know where you're going, absolutely. But if you're always fixated on the finish line, you're going to struggle to get there—and it will always feel a million miles away. Don't dwell on the end goal. Simply keep starting. You only finish by starting. Think about what you can do next to keep moving towards your goal, then start on it the next chance you get.

If you can, be flexible with your goals. Set deadlines and reward yourself when and if you reach them. But if you miss your personally set deadline, so what? You're still much closer to the end. Keep starting, and you'll finish your projects. Then you'll be free to move on to your next project. Or maybe you'll get to go out and perform your works, art or music—flow into that.

You don't have to always be sprinting to the finish line. If that's how the flow hits you, absolutely, run with it. But don't just sprint to sprint. Don't rush. Flow smoothly. Go with the river, not against it. Give yourself small rewards. Let your project build and grow.

The only way to complete any project is piece by piece. It doesn't all come together in one stroke of genius. It doesn't happen like that for even those true one in a million natural geniuses of their craft. How can we expect it to for ourselves?

"What's life going to be like when you're done with this project? What great things will come next?" That doesn't matter. If you have great ideas, sure, jot them down. But otherwise, let the future be the future. Be here. Watch thoughts and find space in between them, and flow.

Plant rewards for when you get to certain steps in the process—reward yourself—entice yourself. Notice when you're forcing yourself. Simply realize it, then come back to the space, and begin.

Use a pull system, not a push system. The pull system makes you naturally want to flow towards your goals. A push system tries to somehow force you past your goals. The push system is like trying to get behind yourself and shoving yourself onto the task, but your feet dig into the ground because no one enjoys being forced to do anything. So why treat yourself so harshly? Besides, it's unproductive.

Of course, you don't do your best work when you're forcing yourself to do it. You dig your feet into the ground like you've always done when someone tried to force you to do something you didn't want to do. Like when you were a child, and you went limp when you didn't want to go someplace, or you'd run and hide.

Wasn't it always better, and you were more willing to do something if you were offered a reward for doing that something? Like a lollipop or candy bar, a new toy, or simply a trip to the playground? I bet you were much more willing to do that thing or go to that place. That's why the pull method is so much more effective. Entice yourself. Gift your inner child. Yes, even for projects and art that you absolutely love. What's that saying? "Treat yo-self."

Give yourself little reasons to complete your work. Give daily and weekly rewards, or rewards for sections completed. Whatever works best for you at any given moment.

You'll naturally want to flow into your work when you're getting enticed to do it. You'll have no reason to resist—your walls won't be up—your feet won't be dug into the ground—your inner child won't be resisting the work. You'll simply flow into your work. You'll find the space. You'll begin. You'll flow.

With the pull method, beginning will get easier. There will be very few blocks in your way. You'll be ready to jump into your work whenever you choose, be it five or six times a week, once or twice, or a couple times a month. However much time you choose to give to your creative projects, give it. Flow with it. Find some space, get back to that blank slate, and begin. Then reward yourself after you reach a goal. These rewards need not be monetary. It could simply be going for a little walk, doing some yoga, laying in a hammock, or anything you can think of. Entice yourself. Breathe. Find some space. Begin. Flow. Reward yourself. And repeat until the project is complete.

Multitasking Ideas & Projects

To be proficient at multitasking several projects, simply find a little space between each project. Perhaps take a five, go for a walk, do a quick workout, use a method, or simply do some deep breathing. Then jump into the next project as if it's your only project. Find a little space between the two instead of jumping back and forth so quickly. Then you won't be worrying about other projects while working on this one. Your thoughts will be focused only on your current project.

When multitasking projects, find a little space between them. It will make for a much smoother transition from project to project. Find space beyond thoughts of the last project, then jump in and flow, fully focused on this one project. Be only with this project and flow with it. Then, when you're ready, find a little space and flow into the next project. Flow in this moment, focused solely on this project. Breathe and flow.

Once you finish work on one project, again, find some space and begin on the project that needs your attention. If you can find a little space between projects, you'll have a much easier time when multitasking any number of projects. And of course, keep yourself organized with different projects under different folders and all of that jazz. But you know that.

When you're focused solely on one major project, allow yourself the creative freedom to do some minor multitasking. Don't always be so entirely focused on one project, that if a great new idea pops up, you don't do anything with it. Don't let a new idea get in the way of your main project, but you can still get the basic idea down. It could perhaps turn into your next main project.

If some great new idea pops up for another project, run with it, let it happen, write it down, record it. Flow with it. Write it down, play it, draw it, design it. Just go with it. You may be able to get the whole gist of an idea down in 20 seconds or a few minutes, then you can get back to your main focus.

Whatever happens in that first moment when a new idea is flowing doesn't matter. That's not going to be the end of it. It's just the beginning. Let it flow through you, jotting down enough of the idea to remember it later. Then you'll be able to run with it and fully develop it when you choose. The basic idea is there, so you'll be free to run with it any direction that feels right. When you're ready to fully develop that idea, it will be there waiting for you. You won't have to remember anything about it.

Once you quickly get down that new exciting idea, your mind won't get in the way as you dive back into your main project, as your mind no longer has a need to cling to the idea. You allowed it to flow through you, and you captured the idea down in some form for later use. Then, find some space again, jump into your main project, and flow.

You'll learn to trust in your ability to jump from idea to idea, project to project—and you'll know how much info you need to get down to fully develop any new idea at a later time. Plus, you'll know if it's an idea you'd care to develop or not. And if not, you'll simply let it pass and continue with your current project.

If it is an idea you'd like to develop, you'll be able to write down the entire idea in one sentence or paragraph. Or quickly make a sketch or recording to come back to later. Then you're free to jump right back into your current project. And once it's finished, or you have some extra time, you can really start developing the new idea.

Sometimes, if a new idea pops up while working on your main project, it's nice to just go with the flow wherever it takes you, even if it's out on a tangent. Tangents can be great, and just what you need to move the story or project along. Or maybe not. Either way, capturing it in the flow can be valuable—or not. That's your decision. I often do run with a new idea. Yet, I'm pretty good at flowing on the task at hand when I choose, and into the structure that my left has brain has laid out.

Perhaps an idea just needs to flow out of the way so that you can flow where and how you choose. It's okay to flow with even "wrong" ideas. You can even learn to turn them into something interesting or useful. Regardless, it will probably help you flow into your main project once it's out of the way. Once you have, find some space, breathe deeply, jump into your current project and flow.

Don't allow your mind to get so attached to new ideas you'd rather be working on, that they distract you from your main project. That's why I like jotting down new ideas in my notes in a particular folder so that my mind won't have a need to cling to them. The ideas are there to come back to whenever I choose, so my mind has no reason to attach to the idea.

If it is an idea worthy of being developed in the future, you'll have everything you need to begin it later, perhaps even that night after you complete your main project's goal for the day. Then, you can keep building upon it, and it will be fully ready to go once your current project is completed.

New ideas shouldn't be a constant occurrence. When you're working on your main project, you won't want new ideas popping up all the time. And when you're focused and in the flow, they won't be. You won't have to worry about new ideas getting in your way. Your focus will be too strong for that.

It's really at night or at random times when these new ideas often pop up. If you want to, flow with them. Jot them down, perhaps develop them a bit. Then, set the idea aside and enjoy the time off. Enjoy your rewards and time away from your project or any work. Enjoy the company of others and all of life.

With music, absolutely multitask projects, if just for fun. Do something totally experimental with a side project; maybe write a totally off the wall song from time to time; or record something silly, even a kid's song.

Paint something ridiculous. Bring a little humor into your art from time to time, even if you feel you're this totally serious artist. A little laughter goes a long way.

Create something surreal. Go beyond the norms. Just see what happens. Projects like these can really bring new and wider perspectives to your main projects. You'll learn which boundaries to flow into from project to project. Such as, when writing an adventure kids movie versus a crime and drug-infused action-comedy—a TV pilot geared towards a network versus cable—a novel versus non-fiction—or a jazz band versus a pop band.

These other projects will help keep the flow free-flowing into your main projects. The more you flow, the more you flow. And when you know how to find space, sit down with your work and begin, you can aim that flow at whichever project you choose.

So, don't be afraid of multitasking projects. Having a couple side projects may help keep your creativity fresh and flowing—perhaps even something in a totally different creative field. If you're a painter or graphic designer, try making some music or writing—try photography or videography—simply anything to help keep the river of flow running.

Allow any new ideas to flow through you. You're a creative. Allow yourself that freedom. It doesn't need to take up more than a few minutes to get the gist of any new idea down. Then you can jump right back into your current project with a renewed vigor, as you allowed this new idea to flow through, which you're excited about, and that excitement may allow the flow on your main project to be stronger.

Don't be afraid of letting go of one project to work on another. You know how to flow, so when you come back to it, you'll simply begin from where you left off with a fresh flow. Letting a project go for a moment to work on another will often allow you to see it in new ways where you can expand it and add a lot of depth. Take a little extra time off during the rewriting process, and you'll really know what I mean.

Whether you want your sole focus to be on one project or multiple projects, flow with each. I tend to have one main project at a time, with a couple small projects I work on from time to time. Do what works for you.

When I'm writing, after I finish a draft on one project, I often like to rewrite the draft of another, which gives me a little extra time/space between drafts, so I can see it with a fresher set of eyes.

During rewriting, when I have a lot of changes or things to add to a project, I'll usually continue the drafts back to back while the material's fresh—so I don't lose my current perspective. Then in a later draft, I can take a little extra time between rewrites to regain a wider perspective.

The more projects you complete, the easier it will be to notice the difference between ideas you may want to develop later and ones you never will. You won't waste your time with the latter. You'll only jot ideas down that you may want to actually follow through with. Then, simply find the space beyond the idea, or any thought, and jump into your main project and flow.

With multitasking, as always, do what works best for you.

This chapter's a little sloppy, but I decided to leave as is. Multitasking can get a little sloppy if you don't find space between projects—if you don't let yourself get back to that blank slate where you can concentrate fully on the project at hand.

Simply find some space between projects and flow.

Where You Create Matters

Finding a place to work where you can easily flow could help you unleash your creative potential. Perhaps you like working at home, and it's where you flow best. Or maybe you prefer creating in a more vibrant environment. Being able to work anywhere is great. However, distractions can be... distracting.

If you create and work at home, try to make a little haven for yourself—a place without distractions—be it your kitchen island, a corner in your bedroom, or even putting up a makeshift curtain-wall. Try to make it a space in which you only do your creative work in. Where when you enter that space, all you do is create—even if it's just a desk.

If possible, try not to work in the same room you kick back and relax in, as it can be a lot easier to get distracted in that room. If you are working in the same room you hang out and relax in, you're likely to have an urge to watch TV or play on your phone for hours instead of starting on your creative work.

You're also likely to have a nagging feeling of needing to work when you're trying to relax. At least that's how I feel about it, which is why I typically prefer separating my creative space from my living space or going someplace to create. Choose what works best for you—alternate it. And by all means, if you do work great in your living room in front of the TV, go for it. Flow where and however you flow best—and where you can get started quickly.

I've realized that I typically work better away from home. I get plenty of ideas and develop them, but it's more difficult for me to focus on writing at home. That's where distractions lay for me. Places with noise and outside distractions is where I tend to do my best work—at coffee shops or co-working spaces where there's people, music, and sounds all around. For some reason, that's where I can typically really dig in and get my work done—where starting is easier—by removing myself from my normal distracting environment. They're vibrant environments, where my flow is free to roam. At home, I can turn on the TV, read some articles, play guitar or a video game.

Our mind's are used to rambling at home and bouncing around the walls. When you go someplace to work, you may find that you can simply dive right in and get started. Once I step foot in that place, I begin working. It's similar to going to the gym versus having a home gym.

Some people are great with a home gym. I was not one of them. Going to a gym, I'd be about ninety-five percent more likely to get a full workout in and actually push it; versus working out at home, where I struggle to do more than one set of anything. Similar to my preference to run outside rather than sticking to a treadmill—I'm not a hamster.

It's nice to mix it up and create in different places. Write, paint, or play guitar on the porch or in the back yard. Draw or write outside, at the coffee shop, or in the park. Take photos outside of your typical habitats. Create in a new art form or one you haven't done in a while. Simply create. Create in new and interesting places, at different times.

Wherever you create, your phone can be a huge distraction. When you get the urge to check your phone, just realize that urge. Then turn back to your creative work and keep creating. Then, that urge to check something on your phone will diminish, because you've broken the addiction, or at the very least, weakened its hold on you. Leave your phone in another room if that helps.

If your mind seems distracted, do some deep breathing. Feel any tension and breathe into it, dissolving it. Find space behind the tension, beyond and between thoughts. Breathe fully, expanding your belly, chest, and back as you inhale. Then exhale completely.

Find a little space with your breath, and distractions will disappear, regardless of where you're working. Your mind will be clear to focus on your creative work, and you'll flow. Be the vast blue sky—breathe—float—and begin. Flow into your project, or begin developing a new one.

No Need For Seclusion

It's tempting to get so into your projects that you begin blowing off other things you enjoy and secluding yourself. However, secluding yourself is not going to help you be more creative or prolific. Get your work done, but don't stop living life just because you're creating. How would you keep your zest for life? How can you maintain the flow if you're not living your life and enjoying the company of friends and family? Don't save it all for some future time, when you've completed enough work to finally take a breath. Don't deprive yourself of things you enjoy.

In fact, use those things you enjoy doing as rewards for the work you do—pulling you towards your goals, rather than causing you to procrastinate by depriving yourself of things you enjoy. Flip it around so that they entice you towards and through your goals.

Plan fun things to do. Work around them. Reward yourself with them. It will breathe new life into your work. It will make it more alive. It will make you more alive. Live and flow. If you stop living, sooner or later, you're going to stop flowing. Accept that you are not a machine. You're a living, breathing work of nature's art. Live it. Breathe it. Explore. Do things you love. Find new things you love. Exercise. Get out there and live it up. If you like to drink with friends, drink with friends. If you like to run, run. Even if you don't, run anyway.

Don't delay gratification into the future. You should be celebrating life now. Enjoy the little things. Hang out with your friends and family. Exercise. Actually taste your food instead of huffing it down like a mad wolf (I'm not very good at this one, I devour). If you delay gratification, there's a good chance that if it ever does come in the form you're waiting for, you'll have a much harder time enjoying it. You'll lose the art of living, and without that, what's your art going to really be?

So get out there—even if there's some fear—the fear is good. If you can use the fear and move through it, you will start feeling unstoppable in your life and not just in your creativity. And you should feel unstoppable in all facets of your life. Do I ever let fear get in the way of my life? Of course I do. But I sure feel a lot better about things if I move through the fear and do it anyway.

If you can let your inner child roam freely from time to time, it will be easier to bring that freedom into your creativity. Don't think that you've got to be mister or miss serious and perfect all the time. Imperfection is where life often really lies—in the cracks. That's what connects us, and it's also where we can share a lot of laughter. And laughter is one of the great human connectors. We could all use more of it.

Let yourself be you without trying to keep yourself within these certain lines. Follow your heart, instincts, and flow. Freedom is needed when you're a creative. Free your creative self. That's why writer's block is such a big thing. If you have writer's block, you're probably not giving yourself enough freedom—creatively or generally.

"This has to be great. Why isn't this working? What's wrong with me? I have to do this. Until I finish this, I won't be able to enjoy anything. If I could just do this one stupid thing, I would be done with it." Screw all that noise. Get out and live. Stop forcing yourself into one space and only one space. Go for a walk. Work on something else. Listen to music that makes you happy. Hang out with friends. Call an old friend. Do some yoga.

Find flow somewhere else in your life and bring that energy into your project. Not by forcing it, but by allowing it. If you're blocked, you're forcing—you're too stuck on one thought, one outcome—on perfection.

Stop forcing. You do that by watching—by noticing the fact that you're forcing. Don't forcibly stop forcing—allow the forcing to stop by noticing, by observing the force you're exerting. Simply observe it. Be the vast open sky. Watch the pressure drift away and dissolve like any other thought. Watch the cloud pass. It will pass. Don't follow it. Allow it to pass. Breathe into the open space.

Watch the storm—your mind's mad searching, unending thoughts—the thunder and lightning. Find the space and freedom behind those storms. Let the rain fall.

Now jump into your work—simply begin. Feel that creative drive. It wants to flow. Mind wants to flow. Allow it. Life wants to flow through you, through your mind, and into your creative projects. It will. You've created the space to allow it. So jump in, right brain, or left. If you've got your work structured and ready, dive in with your right brain and fill in the space—flow through it.

If structure needs to be built, let your left brain flow into structure, into outlines and development. Then take a moment, get back to the space, and jump back in with your right brain to fill the space. And if none of this makes any freaking sense, good. You're probably ready to just hop into your work and flow with it. What's stopping you? Absolutely nothing. So set this book down and begin. If you need some more motivation later, pick it back up, grab another book that inspires you, or perhaps The Now Habit. Use a method, any method. Find some space, breathe, begin, and flow.

Find your inspiration. Find some space and flow. Let it happen—it will. Just rest in the space and breathe a few deep breaths, and you will flow. Just reading this silly little flow right now may be opening the flow in you—or maybe not. Who cares? Jump in, and I bet you'll find your flow. All it takes is one little action step and you can begin flowing on your project right now.

I was certainly flowing when I wrote these few paragraphs and I wasn't even trying. It was just happening. Does it make total sense? Probably not, and I almost hope not, because that's not the point. The point is to find the flow, and you do that by simply allowing it to happen, by finding some space, or just by starting on your project this very moment. Reading this may create that space, deep breathing may, stopping your breath for ten to twenty seconds may, watching the sky may, or simply jumping into your work may. Regardless, you will find your flow. All you've got to do is take that first simple action of starting your project, simply turning to the page you're working on.

You are totally capable of flowing and creating your art. We want to see it. Bring your magic into the world. Why are you delaying? Don't let mind delay you. Use the fear or nervousness or any procrastination—feel it fully—breath into it—move through it. Let the butterflies eat you alive—that would feel amazing. You're here. Do your thing. Be explicitly you. Breathe. Find a little space. And begin.

Use any fear or anxiety you may feel—move through it by beginning work on your project at this very moment. Then the fear will dissolve and lose its hold on you—you'll be free. All it takes is doing one tiny little creative task. Or even simply opening the project and going over where you left off—you'll likely to start flowing right away.

Why not give it a shot this very second?

A Day Off

If at all possible, take at least one day off from your project a week. It's simply easier to keep the flow going if you do. Taking a day or two off allows you to come back fresh with a renewed vigor. All work, no play, makes creativity dull. Get out and live your life.

It could be nice to vary your days off, if possible with work and other responsibilities. Changing your schedule up a bit every once in a while can help keep your flow fresh. Routine can become mundane, causing your creativity to feel the same.

Get your work done, but don't pressure yourself to get it done. Reward yourself with free time and things you enjoy doing. Go camping, to a museum or a movie. Allow yourself to enjoy time off with zero regrets or judgements. You've completed some good solid work and you deserve some time off.

Now flow with your free time. Or don't—just rest. Be fully immersed in whatever you're doing. Don't think that you have to work every single day or always have your project on your mind.

Allow yourself freedom from work. Allow yourself freedom from force. Allow yourself a little peace, a little zen. Take an extra day off, with no thoughts of work or your project. If you have thoughts about your project, just watch them. Then continue enjoying whatever you choose to do on your day off.

Then, the next day that you choose to work, you'll be ready to begin again on your project, and your flow will be new, fresh, and free.

Sometimes I will write for a couple hours on a Sunday. Then, almost like clockwork, I notice that I don't have as strong of a drive to get going on Monday or the rest of the week. When, if I take Sunday off and simply enjoy it, I come back ready to go and jump into the flow on Monday.

You can still get into the flow without taking a day off—and some weeks you may have a tight deadline where it's essential to work every day. However, if you continue that for more than a few weeks, you're creative drive will likely weaken. And you won't be as excited to jump in or keep going, making it more difficult to start and to flow.

Bring some zen into your creative life and take an extra day off this week.

Don't Be Afraid To Lose It

Don't be afraid to lose your creativity, skills, or your flow. You'll always be able to come back to the flow. If you're not flowing, just notice. Don't judge. Accept that you're not flowing well right now. Don't fight it. Your mind's probably just crowded with disrupting thoughts about why you're not quite ready, or you're not good enough, or "who am I to try to make anything, to create?"

You've become too connected with the mind, with thoughts, with the clouds. Find some space around your thoughts, then the flow will find you again. Start your creative work and see if the flow doesn't just catch you. Instead of giving into those negative thoughts, sit down and start your work.

Take the power back from your mind. Watch your thoughts from an omnipresent view. Get back to that blank slate, back to the space, to the vast blue sky. That's where the flow will find you and flow through you—where your creativity is alive—where you can focus fully and flow.

If you're struggling to flow, you've likely become attached to thoughts. It happens—it happens a lot—all the time. Just notice when it does. Notice the attachments. Watch them. Watch as your mind attaches to a thought and won't let go until it's resolved or moves on to another thought it must follow.

Find some space between thoughts. Allow the space to open up. Do a method if you feel it would be helpful. Then come back to the space and forget the method. Methods are tools to help you flow whenever you choose. Take some deep breaths, expanding your belly and chest fully, and begin your creative work. Jump into your work, and the flow will hit you.

You'll forget all about any worries, or skills you think you've forgotten, or of losing your creativity. Because you'll be flowing, you'll be creating. You'll be channeling your old skills while continuing to learn new ones and new techniques, styles or subtext to infuse into your projects.

Take an extra day off if you'd like. Take a week or a month off, or even a year if you really feel like it. Perhaps you want to try a new creative venture for a year. Don't be afraid that you'll lose your skill or creativity. It will most likely enliven it. Like how I would feel extra motivated in baseball when I was younger and the spring rolled around after having the fall and winter off, and I had gotten bigger and could hit the ball further. That is until we had to start playing year-round in high school, which is when I stopped caring for the game. It became a chore, not a joy or a place to let loose. It became a force, not a flow. When before, it was where I flowed best. But the flow was forced to stop, so I flowed elsewhere.

Take some time off if you feel like it. Focus on another creative project for awhile. Even just taking an extra day off could enliven your current project. I should have probably taken an extra day off the week I wrote this chapter. Yet, I was still able to flow into the project, even though I was halfway exhausted. I was still having a pretty swell creative day—almost dreamlike, which was kind of refreshing.

Just go with however the flow may be flowing. Don't force it. Don't force the flow to be faster. Simply begin your work and flow. Also, don't force others. Help them flow, even with tight deadlines—it will be a much better experience all around. Let creativity be a joy. Don't force it. Complete your projects. But do that by starting, by flowing, not by forcing yourself or others to get things done—a reward laid out at the end of the tunnel could be just the ticket.

Taking time off can often be comparable to a winter's snow. When spring comes—when you jump back in and start creating again—your focus will be like the sun melting the snow, and the river will flow. Time off allows the flow to replenish. Even a long weekend can have this effect. Perhaps even a slow and easy-going morning—just float the morning through with zero effort. Then noon, early afternoon or evening, begin. Just float gently into your work. Let it flow at the pace it flows.

A gentle flow could be just what your project needs today. Mine did. I was trying to rush a project that needs zero rushing. So my slow day was helpful. Perhaps that's precisely what you need.

What does your project need? Focus on one tiny aspect that you can do now—one little thing—and do it—slowly—flow with it—be easy with it—do that one little aspect. Then perhaps that leads you to flow into other aspects or further expand upon that one. Just start. Focus only on that one aspect and see what happens.

Let it flow. Let it be easy. Float. Breathe. Zero effort. Just go with it—sitting on a raft in a slow drifting river—water perfectly clear, unstirred from incessant forcing—relaxing with zero effort. Let your flow be an almost effortless creating, which can be a very nice change of pace from the hectic overflowing. Enjoy both.

Flow with what's flowing. Accept the nice gentle river. Accept the rapids. Go with it. Begin and flow. Or take the day off. Whatever you feel like, go with it. Choose to begin. Or choose to do something else. Or choose to rest. Float into whatever you choose—flow into it—zero effort. Just start going over where you left off and see what happens.

Time off will only make your flow stronger and fresher. You'll come with new ears, new eyes, new vision, new enthusiasm, new flow. The key is, when you choose to, begin. Come back to the space, and start. Don't force. Just sit down with your project, begin, and your natural instincts will kick in and you will flow.

It may be slightly harder to start after time off—that's fine. Just know that once you start, you'll flow. You've felt the flow, and you can find it again. Don't let a little negativity or self-doubt throw you off. Feel it. Observe it. Then, it will dissolve. Simply take several deep full expansive breaths, and begin. Keep starting and you'll catch a rhythm. It may take a moment for it to click, but when it does, starting will become much easier and your procrastination levels will plummet.

Creative Non-Attachment

When you're away from your creative work, try to remain unattached to it. If some great idea about it comes along, sure, jot it down. Just try not to always let your creative work hang over you. When you're not actively working on your project, allow yourself freedom from it. If you let it hang over you, it will become a cloud that blocks the flow in the rest of your life. Work on your projects when you choose to, not when you're enjoying other aspects of life.

Your mind's likely to get stuck on some aspect of the project or idea and never want to let it go, even when you're trying to do other things. But how are you supposed to enjoy those moments when you're still thinking about some project or task? If a great idea pops up, jot it down. Then move on.

Sure, the project's important, but if you're not currently working on it, why would you want it on your mind? You probably don't, but maybe you're unable to get rid of it. Shaking it off won't work, nor trying to deny it or trying to force it away. So, simply accept it. Accept that those thoughts are there. See how your mind's attached? Watch the attachment. Observe it. Feel it. Spend some time with it, not thinking the thought, but watching how the mind holds onto it. Observe the mind's clinging.

The harder you try to force a thought away, the tighter your mind will likely cling to it. I'd say to simply let it go, but letting go is the most impossible thing to do. You can't just let go. Tell someone to let go, and they'll hold on tighter. The only way to let it go is to see, watch, and feel the connection, the clinging. Then it will dissolve. The grip will release. Then you'll be able to enjoy those moments with friends and family more because you won't be so attached to your work. You won't constantly be thinking about your project when you're away from it. Then when you're ready to begin again, your project will be there waiting for you to start from right where you left off.

Creative Zen is not about shutting mind and thoughts out. It's about freeing your mind and creating the space to focus on the task at hand, which allows the mind to be fully immersed in your project. Don't stop your thoughts. Watch them. Watch how frantically your mind jumps around at times. Perhaps there's some thought from yesterday that it's latched onto, or some upcoming event that you're nervous or excited about. Just watch those thoughts, those threads. Don't get attached to them. Watch the thoughts pass by like clouds in the sky. Stop following them this way or that way. That's how they grab you and take the reins.

An unwatched mind is kind of like a moth to light. It's going to get stuck on every thought that passes through it. It will follow it until another light comes by, and it will follow that one. Don't get so hooked. Don't be a moth to light. Simply allow the lights, the thoughts, to pass. Be zen about it. Thoughts are no big deal, quit taking them so seriously.

Simply find space behind the frantic mind—come back to that blank slate—and you will flow into whichever aspect of your life you choose.

Try going outside on a clear day and look at the sky, lay on a blanket. And when clouds come, remain with the sky, don't follow the cloud. Let the clouds pass. Or go to a waterfall, and instead of letting your mind follow the water down, watch one spot on the waterfall. Let the water fall around that spot, continuing to refocus on it as the water falls around. It will almost feel like it's washing over you and all of your senses. Let the water fall and flow around that spot. And there you are, at home in the calm center in the middle of all the chaos.

Beyond Judgement

Stop judging yourself for where you are with your creativity, or in your life in general. Just accept where you are, plant some creative seeds, grow some roots, enhance your skills. Keep flowing and creating.

Simply start and keep starting, and you'll get to where you want to be. Allow your creativity to be a flow. Try not to force it. Enjoy the journey, not merely longing for the destination. You may reach it, you may not. The only way to know is to begin, to get started. Accept where you are, and go from there. You may even find a new and more fulfilling destination along the way.

Judgements create blocks. Don't let them get in your way. Instead of fighting any judgement, simply accept it. Just feel the judgement, perhaps even what it's judging. Perhaps the judgement is totally invalid, or maybe there's some truth to it. However, if you can flow with your work, the judgements will disappear, along with any reason for them. You'll continue to improve and expand your creative capacities and problem solving abilities.

Once you're able to access flow by simply sitting down with your work and getting started, judgements will vanish. Even if any judgement does creep in, you know that you're beyond them. Judgements are merely thoughts. Find space beyond them and flow, then the judgements will float away. When you're flowing, there can be no judgement.

Stop judging your days, or your creativity on any given day —your output, frustration, lack of motivation, or skillset. Accept it. Don't fight against it. Go through it. Feel it totally and find space within it. Let it dissolve by simply watching it and breathing deeply. Let the space grow. Watch it overtake any fear, lack, frustration, or tension. Breath overtakes it fully and dissolves or melts it away. Then the flow is fully free to stream through you. Breathing deeply and following your breath clears the junk from the space and you're back to a blank slate.

Instead of judging where you are in whatever creative endeavor you may be working on, improve, get better at your craft. Learn a little more about it. Flow into the learning. Don't try to memorize anything. Just flow with it, and any memorization will take care of itself.

For memorization, allow the space for the memory to grow without forcing it. Don't try to grab onto it and store it away. Just repeat or write down what you need to memorize until it flows like second nature. Then flow in new ways with what you've learned. Keep it creative.

If you remember, good. If not, good. That nagging feeling of trying to remember something is quite un-zen and is bound to block flow. Clear your mind of those nagging thoughts and feelings associated with trying to remember. Don't fight to recall something you're trying to learn. If you can recall it in the moment, excellent. If not, you need a little more repetition. Simply, flow with it, and you will remember it after you repeat it enough.

If you force memorization and try to drill it in, you may be able to recall it briefly, but it won't be ingrained in your mind. It will simply be a trapped thought. Free it. Free yourself from having to remember it. Then you can get. back to creating.

Wherever you are creatively, accept yourself, knowing that you'll continue to improve, hone your skills, and find what truly drives you creatively. Keep starting. Keep breathing. Keep flowing. If you can flow into creative projects and keep at it, you will reach where you want to be creatively and beyond. No judgement will be able to stand in your way. You're moving beyond judgement. Create, and keep creating.

Waste Time Freely

Allow yourself to waste time freely. Don't judge yourself for wasting time. Wasting time is one of my favorite pastimes. As long as you get your work done, do whatsoever you may please. It's okay if you don't fill every moment with work or thinking, reading, or learning. Go with it. Waste all the time you want.

Reward yourself with time to waste—enjoy wasting it—waste fully. Then when you want to create, jump in and flow. Then waste more time if you want. If you like wasting time, accept it. Then, once you accept that fact, you'll stop judging yourself when you do waste time. You may even realize that you don't need as much time to waste, as your mind stops telling you that you must complete some other task, and you allow yourself to waste time with zero regrets.

Choose to get your work done. Choose to waste time. Do both fully. Flow with both. Enjoy them both—or not. That's fine too. I certainly don't enjoy everything. But I do enjoy wasting time. And I waste it rather freely. However, sometimes when I'm wasting time, I feel like I should be working on something. That's when stress and tension set in. If you can recognize that tension forming, you can find some space again and move beyond any tension. Feel your arms, jaw, and shoulders relax as you breathe into any tension and it melts away.

Keep starting and you will complete your projects. Enjoy your work. Enjoy your life. Even try to enjoy your day job. Bring a little zen to mundane work, and things will not frustrate you near as much as they normally do. Find some space and those small annoyances will almost be laughable in how little they start to affect you.

Some days, I enjoy wasting time in the mornings before I begin to work on anything. If I have no obligations in the evening, I may just watch TV or lay around and read for a few hours in the morning. Then I'll finally get up, shower, head to a coffee shop, and write.

Even when you're very busy with other work or obligations, you can still do some quality work on your projects. Flow with it, perhaps in shorter increments. An hour of work is a lot more than none, and will get you a lot closer to your project's end goal. Reward yourself afterwards with some quality time-wasting.

Since this chapter's about wasting time, how about for the rest of the day, you waste it? Think you can do that? Waste the day totally. Just say, "Hey, I'm not gonna do nothing for the rest of this day, and it's going to feel great!"

And simply do nothing for the rest of the day. Do absolutely anything you want aside from work.

One day, I dare you to do absolutely nothing—including no TV, phones, or anything. Spend one day like you're back in the early 1900s or before. If you complete this dare, I can almost guarantee you'll find an awesome flow the next day, or even that night. You might just catch some amazing rapids where your flow is unstoppable. Try it—an entire day with zero electronics—no phone, internet or TV—I dare you.

Beyond Criticism

Everyone judges pretty much everything almost all of the time. And most people dislike many, if not, most things. Just because someone doesn't like your work doesn't mean it's not good or that there's not an audience for it. Just look at all the junk out there that people consume. If you can get your work to a certain level of quality—which you do by consistently starting and flowing on your projects—there will be an audience for it. Reaching that audience is another story. That's for the marketing geniuses.

Simply create. Find the flow and continue to find it. Sometimes you'll still try to force your creativity, we all do. Simply notice the forcing and say, "Oh yeah, that's not how this works. That's why I'm getting frustrated. I'm frustrated because I'm trying to force myself to create, which is blocking my flow and creating unneeded tension, causing me to work a lot harder with much less creative output and/or satisfaction."

Go back beyond force. Simply watch and find some space for the flow to spring forth from. Then once again, the magic will flow out. It simply happens. Become an instrument for the flow to flow through—run with it. I hope you've felt that flow, and I hope it continues to grow and becomes easier and easier for you to access.

In the flow, there is no criticism. It's you with your work, in the moment, flowing, and that's all. Criticism disappears. And if it reappears later on, perhaps it's showing you how to make your project better or improve upon your next project. Then you can flow into creative solutions to those criticisms. Instead of letting any criticism get you down, allow them to help you improve. Or simply go beyond them and keep flowing.

If you don't like your creative work, or you're not proud of it, simply learn from it or improve upon it. Rewrite it until you do like it, or use what you've learned to make your next project better. When you're flowing, you'll always be strengthening your craft and improving your various skills. Don't allow any criticisms to dig in, yours or others. Only allow them to be signposts pointing out what you can improve upon—or throw them out entirely and keep creating.

Keep flowing, and your creativity will reach the level you aspire towards. Then there will be nothing left to criticize. Well, not a lot anyway. Nothing's perfect, at least not to everyone. Allow any perfectionist tendencies to drop by simply noticing them. Perfectionism is simply a block, a fear of criticism. Be beyond criticism. Don't worry about it, nor fear it. Simply keep flowing, keep creating, and you'll keep improving. One day, maybe soon, even you won't be able to criticize your work. You'll start to become truly happy with your creations. The only way to get there is by starting you creative work today—right now. Instead of putting it off, take one little swing at your project and see what happens.

It's Okay to Fail

Failing isn't failure, it's growth. The only failure is giving up. If, once you get to the end of your project and you don't like it, and no one else seems to, don't be discouraged. Take a breather and start again on something new. You'll always have newer and fresher ideas, and you'll now be better at developing and following through with them. Your skills have grown, and now you're more capable of seeing the bigger picture and completing projects.

Or, maybe your project just needs another rewrite or edit to make it work? *This one did.* Really be discerning on the aspects of your project that you truly love and others which have kind of fallen flat on you and perhaps others.

Go in without thinking about how to make it better in any way. Simply go in and mark it up, noting the parts that don't excite you or add much to the story, song, or design. Also, note the parts you really do love. Then go back and expand upon the parts you love—rework, replace, or remove the parts you don't care for. Remember, first drafts are never perfect.

Say, you're recording an album and there's a song or two that just aren't working, cut 'em and write something new.

If you're disappointed in your final work, accept it. But don't give up. It's simply a lesson. Push through. Set rewards and goals to pull yourself forward on your next project. Keep starting and flowing, then by and by, you will have full command of your creativity. It will just happen; it will flow and sometimes overflow.

Keep sitting down with your creative projects. Let new ideas flow. Reach your bucket back into the well. Ask yourself questions and let your right brain flow with answers. Build upon the answers and develop structure with the left brain. Flow through and around the structure with your right brain.

Don't allow discouragement to eat you up. Feel any discouragement. Simply accept it. Feel it totally and breathe into it. Then, even in it, you'll be able to find space. You'll realize that not even discouragement can hold you down. It has no substance. It too, is just a thought your mind is clinging to—a block. You're beyond that.

Start and keep starting, keep flowing, and you will get to a point where you'll be happy with your creativity. Simply take some deep breaths, find some space, begin, and flow—that is all. Allow your creativity to flow and getting good will take care of itself.

Method Vs No Method

The idea with using methods is like the master training the student until the student becomes the master. Use the methods until you no longer need them. Use the methods until you're so easily able to access the flow that you become the master. Then the methods won't matter, which is the ultimate goal—to simply jump into your work and flow.

Even then, it's still good to have some methods if you do end up needing them, or if you find yourself working on a project that doesn't excite you. If you're having trouble accessing the flow in general or for a particular project, go back to a method that helps you find space or has helped you flow. Then go beyond the method, and begin. If you need a method, use a method. If not, great. Simply begin and flow.

Deep breathing is something you can always come back to and rely on. Take a few deep full breaths, concentrating on inhaling and exhaling completely. That's really the only method you'll ultimately ever need. It can toss you right back into the space—to your center—that blank slate. Then you're free to flow on any creative task you choose.

If you feel like you need a method, use one or combine a few, or create a new method. Exercise more. Remove the body blocks to help remove the mind blocks. Lay down out under the blue sky and watch the clouds pass by. Keep your attention on the vast clear blue sky. Be the sky. Don't fight the clouds away. Stop allowing your mind to attach to the thoughts. Stay with the sky. Be the sky as the clouds pass by. Just breathe the open air.

Then, when you're ready, jump back into your work and let the flow happen. No force, just allowing, watching, being. Begin, and flow.

Breathe. Breathe deeper and fuller than you can ever remember breathing. Breathe deeply until your breath is smooth and full. Keep breathing, letting your belly, chest and back expand. Breathe full and complete breaths. Then sit down with your project and flow.

When Motivation's Lacking

When you're lacking motivation but there's something you really want to work on or finish, just hop in and do it anyway. Don't force anything. Just sit down with your work and let the flow happen. Look over your project—or pick up your guitar—and see if your mind doesn't take off and run with it. Do one little creative thing.

Perhaps your flow is only a trickle or a small stream today. However, if you can let that little bit of flow happen, if you can start on one small step, your flow might just turn into a mighty river and you blow through your daily goal and far beyond. You never know unless you sit down with your work and get going.

Sure, when you're overflowing, there's absolutely no stopping you. But what's stopping you now? Are you not feeling motivated? Well, what motivated you in the first place? How will you feel when you finish the project? Have you laid out any rewards to entice yourself? How do you feel after a day of solid creative work, versus a day that you decided not to do any work because you just weren't feeling it?

You don't always have to feel it, or be in the mood to create. If you can simply start and focus in on your creative work, you will flow. Find a little space beyond distracting thoughts and your mind will be able to focus on the task at hand. Then your creativity is free to roam, free to flow.

Do you think famous musicians, comedians, actors, or athletes are feeling it every time they hit the stage or go into the studio? Nope, but they make it happen anyway. Sure, some have substantial monetary incentives, but they've learned to perform even when they're not feeling it. Realize that you don't have to be one-hundred-percent-on every time you do your creative work. You can still create something great.

If you're able to sit down with your project, even just for a little while, you will find some sort of flow. It may be a slow flow, or maybe it bursts into rapids, breaking down any walls, restrictions, or sleepiness trying to stand in your way.

Just start. Don't wait. You will find the flow. Maybe this seems contradictory to the whole not forcing aspect of the book. But when you sit down to work, you're not forcing, you're just being there with your project. Begin reading where you left off with your writing or listening to your mix, or where you left off painting or designing. The flow will hit you and you'll instinctively know where to go. Start. Even if you don't feel like it, start anyway, and keep starting.

You've chosen to work on this project. It's something you really want to do, or it's something deep down that you feel you must do. So start. No more waiting around for the perfect moment. That moment is this moment. What aspect of your project can you work on next?

To really get into the flow, finding or creating space in your mind can be important—going beyond distracting thoughts—but you also have to be able to choose to sit down with your work and begin. It's about deciding to start, and following through by beginning your creative work. That's when your flow and creative work become consistent, and how your projects will get consistently better.

When you're not working on your project, don't think about it. If some great new idea flows into you, write it down for when you start your project again, then forget your project completely. Live your life. Enjoy the small and large things.

When you're not working on your project, aim to remain detached from it. If you hang onto your work, it's like a cloud that follows you. Your sky becomes clouded. Therefore nothing new can come in, and it gets more difficult to enjoy your free time or time with others. If you can find some space—the vast open sky—then the passing clouds don't attach to you. Then you're free to enjoy your time away from work. Plus, you're free for new ideas to flow to and through you. You become a beacon that newness always seems to flow and flower through. You're no longer a rock, a wall—you're the sky, the ocean. You're not small and closed off, you're incredibly vast.

Take fives throughout your day. It's unhealthy for your body and mind to sit with one task for over two hours. Fives have become almost sacred to me. Take a short stroll and relax for a moment. Then sit back down and continue your creative work.

After a short break, the flow happens nine out of ten times when you hop back into your project. Fives keep me fresh. Perhaps they'll keep you fresh as well. And maybe they'll help you find a little extra motivation. Maybe even throw a few small rewards in throughout your day for a little extra boost.

Osho talks about bridging the East and the West by bringing a meditative mind into the marketplace. That's basically what this book is about—bringing zen into your creativity, into your work—into the marketplace.

Simply find a little space in yourself, get a little zen, then sit down and do your work. Once you start to get the hang of it, then you can just dive right in at any moment, and the flow will flow.

That's why some days you should just dive right into your work without using any method beforehand, because the flow may be there. You've accessed flow before, at least when you were a child, and probably recently in one facet or another, and once you've felt the flow, it's possible at any moment to jump right in.

Ultimately, no method will be needed to get into the flow. That's where we want to get, but the methods can make it easier—just like with meditation. You'll probably need a method to get you there, but once you've found it, the mind wants to cling to the method and forget where it's gotten you.

Your mind will want to attach to the method. You drop it by finding space beyond thoughts, where you're holding onto nothing—everything comes and goes, ebbs and flows. Be the space behind all the noise. Rest in the space. Take a five and breathe. Then sit back down and jump into the flow of your work and your creativity will be fresh again. This will keep your flow fresh throughout your day, week, year, and beyond. You'll be able to flow at any moment.

The point of the methods is to get you to where the flow comes naturally when you sit down with your work. You won't have to remember some method every day. You'll be able to sit down and start flowing. Don't be discouraged if you're not there yet. Continue finding space through the methods, or deep breathing, then one day, you'll be able to drop the methods.

Here's one last improvised method combo. Try creating some of your own, or continue this one and others beyond what's written (even writing them in the book).

Breathe... Deeply... Slowly...

Breathe every drop of air out... Every last drop, even if you have to push it out. Nothing left.

Now, breathe in... Slowly... Deeply... Fully... Let your lungs, belly, chest, and back fill totally—until they can't expand any more.

Now, let it out totally. Every drop. Smoothly. Fully. Squeeze all the air out.

Allow the breath to flow in—totally filling your lungs—filling every cell with oxygen...

Now, let it all out—smoothly...

Allow the breath to be slow and smooth. Stay with it for as long as you want, breathing in and out completely.

Then, forget it. Simply watch. Feel. Feel any space. Be the space. Breathe it. Be the river, the ocean, the rain. Ebb and flow. Let your creativity pour forth into projects large and small, smart and silly, wild and outrageous, dreamy and surreal. Wherever your ideas may go, flow with them.

Keep starting and keep creating. Start now—today—this moment.

Find some space, begin, and flow.

Get a little zen and create.

<u>Closing</u>

There you have it. If you've made it this far, I hope you've gotten some great work done. If you haven't even begun, well, set this book down and begin. For literally only five minutes, start something creative—zero worries or thoughts about finishing it. Just simply do one tiny piece. Then later on, you can continue it if you feel compelled.

Do one tiny piece now. Write one word, one sentence, one line, one progression. Draw one shape or shade, one carving. Just start. Start, and the flow may just begin to pour through you. Let it. You'll never know until you begin. So start. Now.

The world needs more creativity. It wants you to flow. It wants you to reveal yourself. We all want more creativity. We all want the world to be a better and more beautiful place. Help us out and create your works, large and small.

Keep finding space and flowing, and you'll get to a point where you are a tremendous force. Even if you don't feel like you have any creativity in you, you can find it. You simply haven't accessed it, or you're afraid to try. Don't be. The only thing holding your creativity back is your inability to begin, and perhaps a little fear. Move beyond mind, beyond thoughts, and you'll move beyond fear. Feel any fear. Feel it totally. Find the space around, behind, and inside it—breathe into it—and watch as the fear dissolves.

Then simply dive in and begin, continuing your current project or starting a new one.

You will find your way. You'll find your own flow. You'll find your passions. You'll move beyond procrastination and continue starting. The more you jump in and begin, the quicker the flow will come. It will be tremendous and grand at times where inspiration pours through you. Then there will be days and even weeks where it will only be a small stream. That's fine. During these times, it's often that you may need to allow your left brain to build a little more structure for your right brain to inhabit and flow through. That's when you become the ocean. Your left brain ebbs, the right brain flows, or vice versa. There's the wave, and there's the undertow. Once you get that back and forth flow going, it is tremendously unstoppable.

Allow your creativity to flow freely. It often feels like the world wants to tie you down and throw you into a round or square hole. Perhaps this book will help you untie yourself. I hope so. You deserve creative freedom. Don't box it up. Be explicitly you. That's what we really want.

Keep starting, keep flowing, and you will improve your abilities so much that within a year or two, you won't believe how far you've come. Flowing will be second nature. You'll be making better creative decisions. You'll know where to go and how to get there. Then in five or ten years, you will be a total master of your art. No one will be able to touch you, and you won't have a care in the world if they could.

You're doing your own thing. No one else can do it in the exact way you do it. No one else has had the experiences you've had or the same interests or instincts. You will gain fulfillment from the creative aspects of your life, which will flow into all areas of your life. You'll simply be flowing. You are flowing. Keep at it.

Simply start. Create your art. Do your work. Let your creativity loose onto the world. Let it be free — whatever it may be — no matter how off the wall or strange.

Go for it. Why not? You may just start to surprise yourself. What are you waiting for? Simply begin. Simply start and keep starting.

Breathe—find some space—get back to that blank slate—and begin.

Continue starting and flowing on your projects.

Get a little zen and create.

That is all.

That is Creative Zen.

About The Author

Mark Chaney is a writer, filmmaker, yogi, musician, and photographer. He was born in Austin, Texas, and grew up south of Nashville, Tennessee. In 2004, he began his journey into yoga, zen, and tao, and dedicated himself to living a creative life.